A YEAR IN FIGURE SKATING

ALSO BY BEVERLEY SMITH AND DAN DIAMOND

Figure Skating: A Celebration   1994

M&S

A YEAR IN
FIGURE SKATING

BEVERLEY SMITH

Edited by Dan Diamond

Canadian Cataloguing in Publication Data

Smith, Beverley, date
      A year in figure skating

Includes index.
ISBN 0-7710-2754-0

1. Skating.   I. Diamond, Dan.   II. Title.

GV850.4.S64 1996   796.91'2   C96-931407-8

The publishers acknowledge the support of the Canada Council and the Ontario Arts
Council for their publishing program.

Design by Kong

Typesetting by M&S, Toronto

Printed and bound in Canada

McClelland & Stewart Inc.
The Canadian Publishers
481 University Avenue
Toronto, Ontario
M5G 2E9

1 2 3 4 5   00 99 98 97 96

C O N T E N T S

To Marion Gamble, who taught me more than the key of C

Introduction

During the 1995-96 season, the real world trod noisily upon that ethereal part of figure skating that brings a glow to chilly cheeks, stretches spirals into tender moments, and lets hearts beat to the rhythm of the ages.

After all, there was money to be made, futures to decide, and territories to claim in the name of television ratings. The stakes were as high as a spotlight's eye. To the strong of heart went the victory.

The winners and the strong proved to be the Russians at any level, any discipline, any time, any competition; the Americans regained their power, led by Todd Eldredge, Rudy Galindo, and the transformed Michelle Kwan; and there were distinct hints of an eventual, powerful awakening of the Chinese.

Among the broken of heart, at times, were a frail-looking Midori Ito of Japan, making her amateur comeback after four years as a professional skater; Josée Chouinard of Canada; Surya Bonaly of France; Michael Shmerkin of Israel; Nicole Bobek of the United States; the French team, many hampered

"This is like a dream," said Rudy Galindo, minutes after winning the men's title at the U.S. figure-skating championship. "Yesterday, I just had the feeling I was doing a clean, long program. I kept imagining the crowd standing the past week. I couldn't sleep. I could visualize being on the ice and the crowd standing for some reason. I can't describe this moment."

(Page 1)
Todd Eldredge
(Facing page)
Michelle Kwan

Midori Ito was mesmerizing in early practices at the world championship in Edmonton, but later appeared visibly nervous, even anguished. After she finished her qualifying round, she spent two hours in hospital with an anemic condition, perhaps brought on by a crash diet she undertook just before her first amateur competition outside Japan in four years.

by injury; and talented Latvian pairs skater Elena Bereznaia, who suffered a severe head injury in a training accident in January 1996. And perhaps most broken-hearted of all was skating's charmed treasure, Ekaterina Gordeeva, whose incomparable husband and pairs partner, Sergei Grinkov, died suddenly of a massive heart attack at age twenty-eight on November 20, 1995.

Although the figure-skating season now stretches almost year-round, most of its high-profile successes and tragedies were played out in the arenas of amateur national and international events, which gear up in late August and wind down in March at the world figure-skating championship. (During Olympic years – every four years – world championships tend to be held in late March, to give skaters time to recover from the experience and stress of a Winter Games.) Skaters in the professional world perform whenever there is a

Famous Russian coach Tamara Moskvina took over the training duties of Latvians Elena Bereznaia and Oleg Shliakhov in May 1995. She smoothed the rough edges of a very athletic pair. "The main focus was to make their skating more clean, with better lines, better harmony, and to put in their programs some artistic movement that will show the elements even better," Moskvina said.

willing promoter, an available rink, and a public eager to buy tickets. But pros tend to be busiest when amateurs are: from fall to the following midsummer.

The very best of the elite amateur skaters from around the world have always hoped for assignments to the top international competitions such as Skate America, Skate Canada, the Trophée de France, the Nations Cup in Germany, and the NHK Trophy in Japan. In the past, these events have served to help skaters show off their wares to international judges, test new programs, and have a peek at what their competitors were doing. They did not qualify a skater for any other competition. But during the 1995-96 season, these five major events took on more significance; they became qualifying events in the new Champions Series of Figure Skating, which led to a final showdown for big prize money. Its final – a new event in skating – effectively

Michelle Kwan earned two perfect marks of 6.0 (from a Bulgarian and a Japanese judge) for artistry in her long program at the world championship, but they were not her first. She had picked up a 6.0 in a Pro-Am competition earlier that season in Philadelphia. "I can't remember girls getting a 6.0," said her veteran coach, Frank Carroll. "Certainly not during recent years."

became a mini-world championship, a February preview of the drama that was to come at the world championship in Edmonton three weeks later.

Other important stops on the road to the world championships are national championships, which serve as qualifying events for world championships. Some European nations also use the European championships to determine which skaters to send to the world championships.

A new event on the amateur calendar was the Centennial on Ice competition in St. Petersburg, Russia, which took place the week before the Champions Series final. It served as a celebration of the one hundredth anniversary of the world championship, which first took place in St. Petersburg in 1896, offering only a competition for men from three different countries. The 1996 event attracted an impressive array of international skaters in all disciplines. Canadian skaters did not attend the event, which was held only a week after their national championship.

In 1995-96, the high profile of skating continued, bringing with it an unabated onslaught of skating events, including the new Champions Series final, five open competitions that mixed amateurs with professionals, more innovative professional events, even-higher television ratings, and other things – good, bad, and ugly. One of the ugly things touched the delightful innocence of Michelle Kwan, a fifteen-year-old gamine with an unbeatable consistency and a delicate, refined air. To meet her gaze in mid-performance is to feel you have been brushed by butterfly wings. Still, somebody threatened her with death.

Although Kwan had been a prime subject in the dark heart of a man in turmoil for about a year, the issue became public at the Champions Series final in Paris in late February; the man who threatened her lived in Paris. Kwan's peers had no inkling of the danger, even by week's end. "He is someone that is not well," said Kwan's coach, Frank Carroll. "He's a little, strange man that has written many letters, made many calls."

It started with a phone call, then letters, and "it just escalated," Carroll said. "I guess he's been very, very aggressive, to the point that before we left, the FBI knew about it. He's been very persistent with all the associations in trying to get hold of her. He went through the U.S. State Department, through the French [skating] federation, the United States Figure Skating Association, through Ice Castles [Kwan's training center in Lake Arrowhead, California], everywhere."

Carroll said he has never seen any of the letters. Kwan was told of their existence. But French authorities were "very much aware of him," Carroll said in Paris. "They know where he is at every single moment. He's being watched the whole time she has been here. The whole situation has been very well handled."

The morning of the event finals in Paris, security officers scoured the spacious Palais Omnisport rink with dogs and bomb-detecting equipment, a harsh dose of reality in a pretty scene. Kwan was surrounded by people twenty-four hours a day. "I have been with her," Carroll said. "Her dad has been with her. She felt very safe and not threatened at all. This is what happens to many celebrities."

Kwan's plight in Paris was a sign of her status as an international star and of the prominence of skating in the public conscience. It may not have been the most comfortable way to find that out.

The International Skating Union (ISU), which represents Olympic and world-championship-eligible skaters, bumped up against the real world, too, bringing in the Champions Series to coax amateur skaters to remain amateur and to offer them some alternative to the proliferation of big-money professional events. But then its officers watched and worried as some of their skaters stretched themselves to the limit, danced every dance, tour, or competition during the season, and reached for every money-making opportunity in careers that are sometimes as short-lived as a match flame. Were they burning themselves out?

The president of the ISU, Ottavio Cinquanta, said yes, and backed his premise with parables, as is his wont. "The most important problem of the ISU at the moment is the calendar of events," he said as he revealed in February that the ISU was contemplating a proposal to put a formal limit on the number of events, including tours and exhibitions, that an ISU skater can do and still remain eligible.

"The fact is that ISU skaters have not skated up to their potential. They have been worn out by the explosion of competitions and events. There is a direct correlation between how well the skater performs to his potential and how financially sound the ISU is in negotiating with television and sponsors. If the skaters are worn out and can't compete, we can't command the same relations with sponsors.

"Some skaters say they are still skating okay. But okay is still not okay."

Cinquanta may have been referring to Philippe Candeloro of France, the 1995 world bronze medalist, who missed most of the 1995-96 competitive

Todd Eldredge,
climbing back
from setbacks

Philippe Candeloro as Lucky Luke, a Belgian cartoon character that was his favorite comic hero as a boy. Judges, however, were not amused. They didn't like his heavily cuffed blue jeans, the hat attached to his back, or the spurs on his boots. Some of these effects disappeared by the world championship in Edmonton. Candeloro sought to have everyone understand Lucky Luke by handing out a slick four-color brochure explaining his choice. Why choose Lucky Luke? Partly because of fun, "just because Philippe Candeloro has 'curved' his legs, like those of Lucky Luke's!" the pamphlet stated.

season with a foot injury that first became apparent during the tour of world champions staged by American promoter Tom Collins in the summer of 1995. Or Cinquanta may have been talking about Todd Eldredge, who slipped to second place at the U.S. championship with a performance that wasn't bad, but only "okay," after taking part in a "Nutcracker on Ice" tour that went through twenty American cities during the month before the national championship. Or Cinquanta could have been thinking about Nicole Bobek, who had to withdraw after the short program at the U.S. championship with an injury that didn't get a chance to heal while she took part in the same "Nutcracker" tour. Or perhaps he was troubled by the tough year of Surya Bonaly, a three-time world silver medalist, who failed to qualify for the Champion Series final that was held in her own country.

Bonaly battled boot problems all year, but some speculated she was simply burned out after years of constant competition and tours – and of training full out like a paratrooper at every session, driven by her ever-watchful mother, Suzanne. Aside from being a major part of the Collins summer tour in 1995, Bonaly also participated in a ten-day set of exhibitions in France directly before Skate America, her first amateur competition of the year. She said she had no time to practice, and finished fourth over all.

During the past year, the ISU sanctioned fourteen major international events, with a sprinkling of other less-high-profile competitions, such as Prague Skate, "but there is a big difference between that and a hundred," said Cinquanta, apparently referring to Collins, a U.S.-based touring mogul who runs a three-and-a-half-month tour of champions that starts after the world championship and ends when snow and ice are long forgotten – in mid-July. For the 1995-96 season, Collins also established a mini-winter tour that lasted about two and a half weeks, directly after the U.S. championship in January.

"I have not mentioned Mr. Collins by name," Cinquanta said as he mentioned Collins by name (when pressed). "He is a friend of skating as long as he realizes that figure skating now is not like it was twenty years ago. The required elements are so much more difficult now that it takes a lot of practice time.

"A sprinter who can run ten seconds must not run eleven seconds. He must run 10.0 or 10.1. Some of our skaters are performing not bad, but not in line with their skills. So my message is delivered to everybody. Anyone who is jeopardizing the skaters' ability to perform is not a friend of the ISU. We have to be tough enough to say enough is enough, too much is too much."

Surya Bonaly,
in a tough search
for success

Cinquanta would get no argument from esteemed American coach Kathy Casey, who says she has nothing against Collins and the money skaters can earn during his tours, but she has some trouble with the lack of training time they have. After all, her student, Scott Davis, and Todd Eldredge both bought their own condominiums during the past year. The tours and opportunities have also afforded skaters money for training, for the best choreographers, for the best costumes and equipment. But it's during the summers – at the same time as the long Tom Collins tour – "where we should be getting our new long programs and choosing our music and learning new things," she says.

Casey makes a strong case for weighing opportunities, opening the financial window just enough to reach a hand through, closing it to buckle down to work again. "Often a small show on the weekend that will make enough money to train for a few months is okay," she says. "But if it's going to take you away for a long time in the [summer or] fall, I don't think that's okay."

Eldredge found this out when he lost his national title after the "Nutcracker on Ice" tour. Both he and coach Richard Callaghan said they would never do it again. Scott Davis and Tonia Kwiatkowski turned down "Nutcracker" offers to concentrate on preparations for the U.S. championship, which determines which skaters will represent the country at the world championship. It worked for Kwiatkowski; in January she took the silver medal at the U.S. nationals in the best effort of her career and earned a berth to the world event in Edmonton in March. It didn't work for Davis, a two-time U.S. champion, who spun out of control, shockingly finished only fifth in the free-skate, fourth overall, and missed a trip to the world championship for the first time in four years.

After the disappointment of finishing second at home to a fresher, well-prepared Rudy Galindo, Eldredge decided to forgo the Collins winter tour and the Centennial on Ice competition. Coach Callaghan estimated that it cost Eldredge more than $100,000 in lost prizes to do so. The time at home didn't help Eldredge at first; he made a tiny mistake in the short program at the Champions Series final in February – he touched a hand to the ice while landing a triple Lutz to catch his balance – and ended up last of six men and fifth overall. But it paid off three weeks later when he won the world title he had missed so narrowly the year before.

Still, Casey is dismayed at what she feels is a drop in the level of high-flying skating skills. "I think amateur skaters are tending to lose their focus a little bit," Casey says. "If you look around at the top dogs such as Philippe

[Candeloro] and Scott [Davis] and Elvis [Stojko], I don't think they've happened to improve at all.

"I think they've improved their ability to relate to an audience and to perform well and to skate for a crowd and to be entertaining. I guess that's all part of figure skating, because they're putting so much emphasis on the artistry mark. I think that part of it is good. But where are the quads? Where are the other difficult things in skating?"

In the past few years, Casey says, there has been a dearth of triple-triple combinations as well. "We've seen a few difficult triple-triple combinations, but you're not seeing a lot. I don't think amateur skating has improved in the last couple of years. I think the lower levels have, and are, catching up to the top."

Casey was itching to see Davis set up a jump combination with a triple loop – instead of a triple toe-loop – as the second jump, but they just didn't have the time to work on it. (Davis left Casey as trainer at the end of the season.) Daniel Hollander and Tara Lipinski of the United States, Jeffrey Langdon of Canada, and Eric Millot of France were some of the few skaters who used the triple loop as the second part of a combination. Millot showed the most difficult of all these combinations when he landed a triple loop–triple loop at the Champions Series final. Such a combination is truly awe-inspiring, because a skater must take off and land on the same foot – without any help from a toe pick or the momentum of a freeleg – not once, but twice. After the world championship in Edmonton, some male skaters hinted they may seek out more triple-loop combinations the next season.

As the ISU watched a few of its stars falling, it found some consolation in its first Champions Series, which was pronounced a satisfying, if not over-whelming, success. "It is not a rousing financial success," Cinquanta admitted. "But we are not in the red numbers."

Still, the series ended up with a $1.4-million surplus that remained after prize money and expenses were paid, with sponsors and networks lining up to sign multi-year contracts in the future, according to Robert Howard, the secretary of the consortium that operated the series in 1995-96. Because the concept was in its infancy, its organizers were not expecting much of a surplus at all.

The financial structure of the first Champions Series represented a new concept for figure skating, with the skating associations of five countries (the United States, Canada, France, Germany, and Japan) forming a business consortium that not only relied mostly on the revenue from sales of television rights, but also on the sale of advertising space on rink boards and from title sponsorship.

The consortium operated separately from the organizing committees that traditionally set up the individual events – all of which had shown an ability in the past to offer well-organized, financially sound skating events. Quickly the consortium raised $6 million for its operations, which included prize money of $232,000 (U.S.) for each of five qualifying events: Skate America, Skate Canada, the Trophée de France, the Nations Cup in Germany, and the NHK Trophy in Japan, for a total of $1.16 million. Prize money for

Jeffrey Langdon,
a plucky Canadian

Oddly enough, both Philippe Candeloro and Eric Millot chose cowboy themes for their long programs. "I wanted to make a program totally different from the tango [his long program from the previous season]," Millot said. "I wanted to show the judges that I can skate everything." Millot says he loves western movies. "I feel like a young kid," he said. His exhibition routine (right) also had a western touch.

Thirteen-year-old Tara Lipinski even inspires Todd Eldredge, who watched her work when she joined his coach, Richard Callaghan, in December 1995. "To be thirteen and to be able to do what she can do is amazing," he said. "She works her butt off. She is already in at nine in the morning. I'm usually just rolling out of bed then. But she'll do her long program over and over and over, and she'll do 90 per cent of what's in it every time. By the time I get my skates on, she's doing her program again." Eldredge is considered a hardworking, disciplined skater.

finishing first in each event was $30,000, with $18,000 for second, and $10,000 for third.

The five international events had each offered prize money on their own before – but not of the amounts handed out by the Champions Series consortium. In 1993, for instance, Skate Canada, for the first time in its history, offered total purses of $28,000 (Can.). In 1994, Skate America paid out $100,000 (U.S.) in prizes to top skaters.

The prize money for the final event in Paris in late February was attractive – $471,000 (U.S.), with a further $271,000 in appearance fees, so that the winner in any category earned $50,000, plus a $10,000 bonus. Only the top six finishers in each of the men's and women's singles events and the top four in pairs and ice dancing made it to this rich finale.

The revenue surplus trickles down to the consortium countries, to the association of the country that plays host to the final, to the ISU, and to associations that were not part of the organizing group.

To match the big-money concept of the Champions Series, the ISU also offered prize money for the first time for its other major events, to the tune of $937,500 (U.S.) for the world championship, $470,000 for the European championship, and $270,000 for the world junior championship.

"Welcome to the business of figure skating," says Canadian official David Dore, a member of the first Champions Series technical committee. It is a new, not-so-ethereal world.

*T*he Road to the Champions Series Final

*F*or the first time in 1995-96, five major existing international competitions on the amateur calendar found a larger purpose as qualifying events for a lucrative final event. Only skaters deemed "eligible" for Olympic or world-championship competition under International Skating Union rule could compete. The ISU designated the five best skaters from the previous world championship in each discipline to two events, but tended to spread the talent around, so that the top contenders wouldn't meet all at once before the final. For a win, a skater would earn twelve points in the race to qualify for the final; for finishing second, nine points; third, seven points; and so on down to eighth place, where a skater would get one point. Skate America, the first event on the series schedule, took place in Detroit, Michigan, from October 26 to 28, 1995; Skate Canada in Saint John, New Brunswick, from November 2 to 5; the Trophée de France in Bordeaux from November 17 to 19; the Nations Cup in Gelsenkirchen, Germany, from November 23 to 25; and the NHK Trophy in Nagoya, Japan, from December 7 to 10.

Josée Chouinard reinstated as an eligible skater after one year as a pro, but without amateur funding. Because she did not compete the previous season, she lost her eligibility for Sport Canada funding. And because she had ceased to be a member of the national team, funding from the national association was in doubt. Chouinard made her comeback when a sponsor, Lubriderm, extended her contract for another year.

(Page 17) Michelle Kwan
(Facing page) Alexei Urmanov

Elvis Stojko remained popular throughout the season. He caused a fan frenzy at practice at the world championship in Edmonton. After he skated, fans flung scores of flowers onto the ice. Because flower girls attend only competitions, a half-dozen rink workers had to leap to the ice in their boots to pick them up. The incident delayed Philippe Candeloro's program, and the rest of the skaters could not practice on ice littered with flowers. "I've never had a practice like that before," said an astonished Stojko. He apologized to the other skaters.

Everywhere Michelle Kwan went, gold medals and dollars followed. Full of bright energy, bouncing from rink to rink around the world with her Mickey Mouse backpack in tow, the fifteen-year-old from Torrance, California, took utter command of the Champions Series qualifying events. Not even a host of Russians (1994 Olympic-champion ice dancers Oksana Grischuk, twenty-four, and Evgeny Platov, twenty-eight) nor their compatriots (pairs skaters Marina Eltsova, twenty-five, and Andrei Bushkov, twenty-six) nor even the 1994 world pairs champions (Evgenia Shishkova, twenty-three, and Vadim Naumov, twenty-six – the only other skaters to win both of their designated events) could match her. Kwan won three in twenty-eight days.

The male skaters were much less consistent than eighty-eight-pound (forty-kilogram) Kwan. Each of their five qualifying events – Skate America, Skate Canada, the Trophée de France, the Nations Cup, and the NHK Trophy – was won by a different skater. Three of the major contenders – Elvis Stojko of Canada, Todd Eldredge of the United States, and Alexei Urmanov of Russia – took turns meeting defeat.

Each of them also had a win: Stojko at the NHK Trophy, Eldredge at Skate America, and Urmanov at Skate Canada. Ilia Kulik of Russia trounced Stojko at the Trophée de France, while Viacheslav Zagorodniuk of Ukraine took the measure of Urmanov and Eldredge at the Nations Cup.

Unlike the male skaters, who took turns defeating each other all season, Kwan hardly knew what defeat was. Under the series rules, skaters could earn points in only two events designated for them by the Champion Series consortium. To test out her new programs in front of a home crowd, Kwan entered an event to which she hadn't been assigned, Skate America, and her rocket ride to an upper-income bracket in the United States had begun. With her three series victories (she won also at Skate Canada and at the Nations Cup), Kwan earned $90,000 (U.S.). That's not counting what she won in the series final in Paris. Add another $60,000 to the sum.

"Michelle now pays a great deal of taxes," said her coach, Frank Carroll. "France takes 15 per cent. Germany takes even more. Then we go home to the United States, and she pays a lot of taxes out there, too. You think you're getting a lot of money, but there are a lot of taxes. There's really not as much money as you think."

The situation is even more severe for Russian athletes. In addition to what the country in which they are competing withholds from their earnings, and what their own government takes, the Russian skating federation claims

Chen Lu had mixed emotions after winning two perfect marks of 6.0 — her first — but still finishing second at the world figure-skating championship. "I feel very happy that I skated very well and got 6.0s," she said. "But I'm disappointed that I'm number two and not number one. There were no Chinese judges on the panel." Her peers gave her a standing ovation at a prize-giving ceremony the next day.

15 per cent of their winnings from international competitions, other than European and world championships. (The Canadian association takes 5 per cent from all amateur competitions, the U.S. headquarters none.) And Russian coaches get another 30 per cent. "It's like tax," Vadim Naumov said. "It disappears."

And even by the time of the world championship in Edmonton in March, some of the Russian and Ukrainian competitors hadn't seen a cent of their earnings; money from Champions Series qualifying events is sent directly to a skater's federation. Skaters and coaches were loath to speak about the problem, fearing reprisals.

Kwan wasn't the only one picking up paychecks around the world. Who was winning when Kwan wasn't? Josée Chouinard of Canada, who had reinstated as an amateur after a year as a professional expressly to take another crack at the world championship; and 1995 world champion Chen Lu of China.

Chouinard won the Trophée de France with her sophisticated-but-delicately-playful programs, while Chen, struggling throughout the year under the weight of her world title, won the NHK Trophy easily, floating over the ice with awe-inspiring beauty and maturity of bearing. Oddly enough, Chen's win in Japan earned her no points toward the final, since it was not her designated event. She earned her way to the series final by finishing second in both Skate America and the Trophée de France. (She narrowly missed winning the event in France; after a dismal short program, in which she finished seventh, she won the long program. However, her disaster in the short prevented her from pulling up far enough to win the gold medal.)

All three – Chouinard, Chen, and Kwan – were packaged expertly: all were athletically able, and all were skating and emoting to music that brought out fine nuances of feeling.

If Chouinard and Chen were settled performers, drawing on previous artistic breakthroughs, Kwan underwent a complete transformation from one season to the next. At age fourteen, and ranked fourth at the 1995 world championship in Birmingham, England, she was a little girl, *sans* make-up, *sans* fashion. But last season, she grew an inch (2.5 centimeters), scooted about the ice with greater speed, jumped higher. And her look changed. Learning from the best, she said, she turned to elegant hairstyles, make-up, and mature themes, like the biblical story of Salome, the young woman who asked Herod for the head of John the Baptist in return for her dancing. Oksana Baiul helped Kwan in the make-up department.

Both coach Frank Carroll and choreographer Lori Nichol used their extensive experience and knowledge of music to put together Kwan's finely tuned packages. And for the first time, Kwan played a role in what she did.

"She loves these pieces," said Nichol, who lives in Canada. "Because she was a part of it, which made it all that much easier. She's so easygoing. In the past, it was 'Oh yeah, I like that. Let's go.' Now, it's 'I really love that,' and she wants to skate something that she really loves."

Carroll and Nichol phoned all over California to locate exactly the pieces of Salome music they needed, after explaining the story to Kwan. "She loved the idea of doing it," Nichol said. "She doesn't want to do the typical thing. She understands, and we've worked on this for many years now. She isn't the

If nothing else, Alexei Urmanov is a fashion plate of another kind. His coach, Alexei Mishin, found a professional designer for a dance group to do his costumes. Last year, Urmanov wore gloves for both of his routines. "It is my style," he said. "It makes me feel more comfortable to put them on." When asked if he would consider programs like Stojko, he said, "I think it's not my style, but I can try if you want. I'm not sure it will be good idea."

cutesy, bubbly kind. She has a depth and a mystery and an exotic side to her that she wants to be able to show.

"And it's wonderful, even though she's young, that she can portray all sorts of characters. It was right from the start. Once we started the on-ice choreography, it was very simple. She was part of it, saying 'Yes' and 'No' and 'I like this and that,' instead of just copying me, which is what she was doing in the past. Then, she looked more like a miniature me than Michelle.

"This past year has been about discovering who Michelle is as an artist. I feel very strongly that she is an artist, a very special artist, and to be able to do that at fifteen, I think shows her capabilities."

If Kwan emerged as a major force in the women's event, Alexei Urmanov re-emerged as one in the men's event after two consecutive years of finishing fourth, off world podiums, even though he had won the Olympic gold medal in Lillehammer. During his first competition of the season at Skate Canada, the twenty-two-year-old from St. Petersburg, Russia, walked the path from rink to hotel in relative obscurity. But by the end of the week, after the audience had a taste of his athletically powerful performances, the expressiveness of his body and arms, and his commanding speed, Urmanov was earning his first standing ovations outside of his majestic home city. Females of all ages rushed down the aisles of the rink to hand him flowers. "I think Canada is one of the best countries in the world for figure skating," Urmanov said. "It is very pleasure to skate here. I will skate here like at home."

The world also saw a new side to Urmanov at the Skate Canada exhibition. He shunned his classical approach and skated wildly, like a rock star, to a Beatles medley. The response was overwhelming.

Urmanov was only one part of the Russian charge that dominated the Champions Series. Russians also ruled the pairs and ice-dancing events, as their custom has dictated over the past thirty years. Although U.S.-based Oksana Grischuk and Evgeny Platov had announced their retirement after the 1995 world championship in Birmingham, their names showed up on lists to enter the Champions Series; because Platov had received treatment that had improved a chronically troubled knee, the couple agreed to maintain their Olympic eligibility (amateur status) until the 1998 Nagano Games in Japan.

Platov had planned surgery for the knee for the summer of 1995, but changed his mind after consulting, among other people, the doctor used by 1988 Olympic champion Brian Boitano. "I had many opinions from great

The other side of Urmanov

doctors in the United States, and they don't recommend operation because nobody can guarantee 100-per-cent success," Platov said. "It can be worse. It can be better. Who knows? Instead, I take time to make some exercise and treatments. Some people fix car. I fix my knee.

"It still hurts, but it is a pain I can skate with now. Last year I couldn't," he said.

After this decision, Grischuk and Platov won everything they entered: a total of nine competitions for the year, including Skate America, the Trophée de France, their national championship in Russia, the European championship, the Centennial on Ice in St. Petersburg, the Champions Series final, the world championship, and a couple of open competitions. They had competed only twice the previous season.

Close on their heels were the arresting new Russian couple, Anjelika Krylova and Oleg Ovsiannikov, who train in Newark, Delaware, alongside 1994 Olympic champions Grischuk and Platov. Skating together only since April 1995, the tall, expressive couple has risen to the top at an almost unprecedented rate: from fifth in their world debut in 1995 to second in 1996 in Edmonton. And they even threatened to push Grischuk and Platov, particularly with their fiery *paso doble* original-dance routine. At the European championship, one judge rated Krylova and Ovsiannikov best in the original dance ahead of Grischuk and Platov.

At Skate America, where the two Russian couples first competed head to head this season, Canadian coach Roy Bradshaw, a product of the great British school of ice dancing, said he preferred Krylova and Ovsiannikov to Grischuk and Platov. "I love [Grischuk and Platov]," he said. "One of their main strengths is their speed and flow over the ice. But they really haven't used their ability. In the original dance, they have gone for too much content, which is stifling their flow over the ice. The original dance didn't breathe.

"[Krylova and Ovsiannikov] are showing much more aggression and expressiveness. The girl is magnificent. She really has charisma-plus."

Bradshaw said the team had improved "tremendously" over their first year of partnership, because Ovsiannikov, who had had less experience in international competition than his new partner, had improved. "Anyone that can equal her expressiveness and talent has to be something himself," he said. "Now there is total balance between the two of them. They blew me away. Grischuk and Platov had better be looking over their shoulders."

During 1995-96, the skating world saw the introduction of a new compulsory dance into all competitions: the silver samba, created by Courtney

Platov and Grischuk,
unbeatable in dance

Finally, Oleg Ovsiannikov struck gold, in a way. Anjelika Krylova is his sixth dance partner. One year, he said, he changed partners three times. "The first half-year was horrible," Krylova said of their new partnership. "Everything was difficult." The Russian couple moved to Newark, Delaware, with their coach, Natalia Linichuk, but always Ovsiannikov's heart was at home in Russia. "He likes Russian music, Russian food. He cannot live without it," Krylova said.

After suffering a serious head injury, Elena Bereznaia left her Latvian partner Oleg Shliakhov (pictured here) and teamed up with Anton Sikharulidze, a world junior pairs champion with another partner. The new pair trained in Colorado Springs with coach Tamara Moskvina in the summer of 1996 and will represent Russia.

Jones, a former world champion from Britain who has in the past been a member of the ISU technical committee. Although it is customary that two of four named compulsory dances be drawn for any competition during a season, the silver samba was mandatory for all dance events in 1995-96. It wasn't exactly greeted with enthusiasm by both skaters and coaches, who considered it too easy.

"It's just a bunch of chassés," Bradshaw explained. "And it's a very forceful dance. The big challenge is to make it compressed to fit the size of the rink. You have to hold back doing it.

"I suggested a few years ago that the most difficult dance be compulsory," he said. "It would be more challenging and beautiful for an audience to look at, and more challenging to the judges. The problem is, you can go the whole competitive season and not do a [difficult] tango. [At Skate America,] there wasn't a lot of speed in the dances. We were asking for a lot of personal interpretation in the silver samba, and I thought I would see a lot more inventiveness and creativity, but even the best of the best are limited by the dance itself."

"Nobody is really happy doing it," said U.S. ice dancer Renee Roca. "It's a bit of a joke."

"It's really boring," said her partner, Gorsha Sur, who defected from the Soviet Union in 1990. "We were trying to spruce it up. We are trying to do arm, head, and body movements, but our feet have to do the dance steps, and there aren't that many steps to do."

Grischuk and Platov were alone in saying the dance was difficult. "I don't think it's easy at all," Grischuk said. "I think some couples doesn't even know how to do more harder, more deep edges. And you have to do it clean. It's fast and it's very hard to do it clean."

"They just skate without any edges, and think, oh, this is easy, easy dance," Platov said. "Nothing to do. But take another dance like *paso doble*, you can see the steps two times more difficult in the silver samba. I like it. It's very fun."

Russians dominated the pairs event, but Germans Mandy Woetzel and Ingo Steuer both underwent knee operations – same knee, same day – in time to skate at the last two Champions qualifying events (the Nations Cup and the NHK Trophy) and make it to Paris. They arrived on the scene with a new style in their programs, choreographed by their friends, Finnish ice dancers Susanna Rahkamo and Petri Kokko, who had retired from amateur competition after winning a world silver medal in 1995. The Finn influence vastly improved the Germans' ability to present their programs, too.

"It's very hard, because it's new for me and Mandy, and new for Susanna and Petri," Steuer said. "They tell us to make these steps, and then you jump the double Axel. We say, 'It's not possible!'"

But a pair that didn't make it to Paris nonetheless played a major role in the series: after a slow start at Skate America, Elena Bereznaia and Oleg Shliakhov of Latvia won the Trophée de France, defeating Americans Jenni Meno and Todd Sand and Russians Oksana Kazakova and Artur Dmitriev, then finished third in the Nations Cup, an event for which they were not designated. The Latvians, trained in 1995-96 by renowned Russian pairs coach Tamara Moskvina, were hot, fast, and more polished than ever. But then Bereznaia, who was growing into a young woman with mesmerizing style, was felled by a serious training injury in January, about a month before the Champions Series final.

Bereznaia, eighteen, underwent brain surgery after Shliakhov's skate embedded itself deeply into the side of her head during a pair camel spin that went dangerously out of synchronization. They were training alone in Riga, Latvia, with no coach to warn them of risks. The pair had gone to Latvia, because Shliakhov had become jealous of the romantic attentions paid to his partner in St. Petersburg by up-and-coming Russian pairs skater Anton Sikharulidze. Shliakhov told Moskvina he wanted to train in quiet surroundings, without tension. Moskvina had let them go, but had to remain in St. Petersburg to prepare Kazakova and Dmitriev for important competitions.

Contrary to media reports, Bereznaia never fell into a coma, but her injury was so severe, Moskvina said, that the girl's speech centers appeared to be affected. By the time of the Centennial on Ice competition in St. Petersburg in mid-February, Bereznaia was out of hospital and attended as a spectator, with a bandanna wrapped around her head.

By the time of the world championship in Edmonton, Bereznaia was back on the ice in Russia, but merely skating around, leaving the fancy tricks to others. "The doctor told her she needs to do movement to help her speech," Moskvina said. "She speaks not fluently."

The January incident caused the pair to miss the European championship, the Champions Series final, and the world championship. It also ended their partnership. In short order, Shliakhov found another partner, a singles skater in Latvia. Bereznaia will skate again. She has been matched with Sikharulidze, who won a world junior title for Russia in 1995 with Marina Petrova. After Petrova and Sikharulidze finished sixth at the European championship in January, they split up, unable to resolve a conflict with a coach. Moskvina said Bereznaia is afraid to skate with Shliakhov again.

Although both Bereznaia and Shliakhov are Russians, they skated for Latvia on the basis of Shliakhov's dual citizenship in that country. Bereznaia does not have Latvian citizenship. Shliakhov will continue to compete for Latvia; when Bereznaia returns, she will probably skate as a Russian.

As the pair rose through the ranks over the past couple of years, Shliakhov became known for his surly attitude. At Skate America in Pittsburgh, Pennsylvania, in 1994, practices were an exercise in unspoken

Mandy Woetzel and Ingo Steuer were plagued with injuries during the season. Both missed events in October because both underwent surgery at the same time on the same knee – the left one. "We are pair partners," Woetzel said jokingly. Later, the pair had to withdraw from Centennial on Ice when Steuer developed a back problem. "The vertebra shifted and the muscle was torn a little bit," he said.

tension. As tiny Bereznaia crumpled to the ice during a fall from a lift or a throw, Shliakhov would turn his back on her and skate away, leaving her to fend for herself. At Skate Canada in Red Deer, Alberta, two weeks later, Bereznaia and Shliakhov came close to winning the gold medal. When they won only silver, Shliakhov refused to attend the medal ceremony. Bereznaia was left to step onto the podium by herself. Canadian pairs skater Kris Wirtz, who won the event with his partner, Kristy Sargeant, gallantly led Bereznaia to the podium.

"[Shliakhov] had a bad temper," Moskvina said. "He was very ambitious, and everything he wanted to do was for himself. The Latvian federation told me that I was their only hope to make him behave differently. I thought this would be a challenge for me, as a coach. He did start to be much better and control his reaction, and he started to take care of her and behave properly. Everybody was surprised at this miracle. Unfortunately, this injury put a stop to this."

Moskvina said she tried to change Shliakhov's behavior by talking to him, giving him examples of proper conduct, and searching for motivations that would work for him. When Bereznaia was hurt, Shliakhov was "scared," Moskvina said.

"I assure you that accident did not happen on purpose," she said. "But he was not careful."

It was a tragic lesson that spread in painful waves around the world. It made qualifying for prize money a secondary goal.

*S*kating in Israel

*A*s bright as the lights are in mid-arena, as beautiful the costumes, as glorious the triple jumps, the skating world discovered in 1995-96 that it is not immune to tragedy. Michael Shmerkin of Israel had to deal with the assassination of his country's leader hours before he was to perform at Skate Canada. But Shmerkin's is a story, ultimately, of hope and personal triumph. His country defied the odds to become a figure-skating nation. Perhaps – if Shmerkin has his way – it will also become a nation of peace.

All his life, Michael Shmerkin has found that freedom is an elusive-but-important state, for he is Jewish and proud of it.

The champion of Israel skates best when he shows his light-hearted, happy soul to the world, mugging to a crowd, bouncing with flashing blade and twinkling eye down the length of a frosty rink. But beneath the comedic surface is an athlete who had to learn hard truths at a young age and who walked a more complicated path to world and Olympic competition than many of his peers, fleeing the Soviet Union and launching the best part of his

After Michael Shmerkin moved from Ukraine to Israel, he visited the Wailing Wall in Jerusalem and pushed a list of wishes into a crack between the stones. One of the wishes was to compete in the Olympic Games. In 1994, in Lillehammer, the wish came true when he became the first skater to represent Israel at the Winter Olympics. Wearing a blue and white uniform with Israel on the back and a Star of David, Shmerkin carried the flag. He was a one-man Israeli team.

*Michael Shmerkin
places his hand
over his heart
during a moment
of silence at the
Skate Canada
international
competition in
Saint John, New
Brunswick. To
his left, behind
the rink boards,
stands Yossi
Goldberg, mayor
of Metulla.
Goldberg acted
as the team
leader at the event.*

career in a warm desert country. The odds have always been against him. Yet he overcomes.

Shmerkin's story is one of the triumph of the heart over war and prejudice — and despite shocking loss. On November 4, 1995, he switched on a television set in his New Brunswick hotel room — five hours before he was to compete at Skate Canada — and was stunned to see the news: his prime minister, Yitzhak Rabin, the messenger of peace and freedom, had been assassinated.

Crushed, he could not see how he could make his feet fly that night. The glaring lights of a rink and the lofty leap of a triple Axel seemed so unimportant somehow. Shmerkin, who had already been impressing everyone all week in his practices, with soaring jumps and quick footwork, wanted to pull out, even though he was in line for a medal; he was in third place after the short program.

"It was a very sad day for all of us," said Yossi Goldberg, Israeli team leader – of a team of one – and a man who considered Rabin a friend after a relationship that had lasted more than thirty years. "No one in our country believes that this could happen." Only the previous month, Rabin had attended centennial celebrations for the northern town of Metulla, where Goldberg is mayor, as an honorary guest.

Even with the traumatic events unfolding thousands of miles away at home, Goldberg urged Shmerkin to reconsider his wish to withdraw. "I said, 'Misha, the best way to honor our prime minister is to skate for the memory of our prime minister.'"

After a moment of silence in the hushed arena that rainy late-autumn night, during which Shmerkin stood clutching his heart, head bowed, the Israeli champion set to work in his glad-rag costume, skating with no small measure of irony to a medley of playful tunes, including "Tea for Two" and, of all things, "Easter Parade." Only toward the end of his program did he waver, but, when he took his bows, the Canadian crowd rose as one, cheering, applauding. "He skated well, but it was not the same Misha," Goldberg said. Shmerkin fought back tears and doubled over, his head buried in his hands, as he faced the wall of noise. It was an emotional moment, when a far-away tragedy forced its bleak undertones on a sporting competition in a tangible way.

Oddly enough, although Shmerkin finished third in both segments of the competition, he was placed second overall, finding silver in his heartfelt tribute, as if wings had carried him there. "I liked that man," Shmerkin said later, speaking of Rabin. "He opened the way to freedom. He was trying to start something new in that region. He was seeking peace in the Middle East. He goes in the peace street. I go in the figure-skating street. I skated because I am Michael Shmerkin. Now I am in shock."

Shmerkin's sadness was profound. He had made a pledge to serve Rabin in the army; he had been allowed to serve in a special unit of the Israeli army that allowed him to mix his sport with his duty near the ice rink. (All young

Israeli men must serve three-year terms.) Shmerkin's military term ended before the 1995-96 skating season. And he also felt doubly responsible for the fate of Israel as head of his family. One and a half years before the Rabin tragedy, he married Sarit, a young Israeli-born woman, at center ice in Metulla. He had taught her to skate.

Israel had not always been his home. Rather, living in Israel had been a lifelong dream of his parents, who worked hard and saved their money in hope of some day escaping anti-Semitic sentiments in the Soviet Union. Shmerkin found freedom first on skates at age four in Odessa, Ukraine, where his mother worked as a model and his father toiled at an electrical company. "When you skate, you can fly. You can be free," he once said. "But then I realize I have no freedom because I was a Jew. They didn't want Jews to represent the flag. You must be Russian."

With this grim knowledge before her, Shmerkin's mother made a courageous move; somehow, she had the paperwork done that suggested she had married a Russian friend, not a Jew. That made her son's path easier. He represented the Soviet Union at four world junior championships, one of them in Kitchener, Ontario, in 1987.

Shmerkin was so small at age sixteen in Kitchener that the rink boards seemed to tower over him. But he was fast and fun and light and free on the ice, and he made his mark by finishing third in the free-skate with an on-ice aura rare for his age group and an unmistakable joy in his tasks. He failed to overcome a sixteenth placing in compulsory figures and ended sixth overall. But he defeated the likes of Eric Millot of France and Steven Cousins of Britain. In those days, his name was Mikhail.

But even though he had finished fourth and fifth in two previous junior world attempts, with medals barely beyond his grasp, the Soviet Union never sent him to a senior world championship. Its talent roster was deep with young boys fighting for international assignments. Shmerkin finished fifth in the Soviet championship in 1989. He was lost in the shuffle.

Pressed by a sense of dread because of their faith, the Shmerkin family emigrated to Israel in 1991 – as soon as the Soviet borders opened up – and joined 650,000 Jewish immigrants, mostly from the Soviet Union, who fled to the preferred refuge of Israel, a country pock-marked by war and terrorist attacks. Staying behind seemed worse, however. Shmerkin's mother was particularly afraid of remaining in the Soviet Union. "It was a situation in which my mother thought something would happen," Shmerkin said. "It was

Jacob Schneider,
director of
Canada Centre

Metulla, with Canada Centre in the foreground, lies in a verdant valley leading to the Golan Heights, seen in the background. It is the winter-sport area of Israel, with snow for only two months.

a feeling in the atmosphere. She was born in 1947 [after the Holocaust], but she grew up in that atmosphere. She felt trauma. It is different for me. I am from a new generation."

Skating and his future in it came second to the family decision. After a lot of thought, Shmerkin decided to pack up his skates and help "build a future for my family." He thought his career was over. "In Israel before I came, figure skating was like camel riding in Canada," he said. The Hebrew language does not even have a word for skating; in Israel, they "slip." At first Shmerkin busied himself with a new, hard life, trying to learn Hebrew, pressing on with his parents, grandparents, and sister, Hanna, who had been a top junior-level table-tennis player in the Soviet Union.

"When you move from one country to another, it's always a lot of problems," Shmerkin said. "It's not like changing a home. It's a new country, with new language, and you have to organize yourself. It was very hard, difficult for everyone. For immigrants who came from Russia, it was very hard because the mentality and the system in life is not the same. To come from a Communist system and to find yourself in a free country! I am like everyone now. I have credit card. I can say what I want to."

And then Shmerkin found Canada Centre in Metulla.

Canada Centre, a large, modern sport facility, was born out of the horrors surrounding Metulla, a town of five thousand at the northern end of the

*Canada Centre,
where flags of both
Israel and Canada
fly. The Canadian
Jewish community
helped finance its
construction.*

verdant Galilee Valley, within feet of the border between Syria and Lebanon, hardly a site for a peaceful existence. In the summer of 1981, the northern part of Israel had been under siege, so much so that three-quarters of the population of the nearby town of Qiryat Shemona packed up and left. "There were only three thousand people left," said Steven Ain, executive vice-president of the United Israel Appeal of Canada, a group that raises funds to rebuild Israel. "Every night people were sleeping in shelters. There were one, two, three attacks a day."

Metulla was one of the towns that faced this barrage of terrorist attacks. On its outskirts is a fence marking the border, piled high with strands of uninviting razor wire. Still, Mayor Yossi Goldberg had a dream; to bring ice sport to Israel. How could this be? Ice sport in Israel, where palm trees wave their jagged branches, and the earth, the buildings, and the hills arise out of the brown dust? Soccer, yes, but figure skating? Many thought the idea was crazy. Goldberg did not. "Israel is not exactly the best country for figure skating," he admitted. "But we have mountains and a ski area near Metulla, although we have snow for only two or three months a year."

When Goldberg dreamed of opening a facility that included a rink, he turned to Canada, whose Jewish community had sent missions to Israel, seeking ways to rebuild a country that had a special meaning to them. "Canadian Jews who give to Israel feel that here is a two-thousand-year-old dream finally coming true," said Eli Rubenstein of the United Israel Appeal of Canada. "It's part of the biblical dream unfolding. People who do not want

to move back want to support Israel from here. They share this dream of rebuilding Israel." When Goldberg asked, he found receptive ears in Canada – but there was controversy.

"Some people [in Canada] thought the whole project strange," Rubenstein explained. "It was too daring, and some thought there were other social needs in Israel that were greater. People who supported the project were going out on a limb."

During the 1980s, the facility was built. Goldberg called it Canada Centre, to show appreciation to the Jewish community in Canada. "Everyone is proud about it," Goldberg said. At its entrance, a Canadian flag flies beside the flag of Israel.

The project has been a grand success. It has put Metulla on the map. It started out only as a basketball court, but it has evolved into a complex with indoor and outdoor swimming pools, squash courts, a target-shooting range, along with an Olympic-sized rink that was opened in 1995, with National Hockey League legend Frank Mahovlich in attendance.

Canada Centre is one of the largest sport facilities in Israel. It has the biggest skating rink in the Middle East and employs numerous people from the sleepy town. And with seven hundred thousand people using it every year – two thousand a day – it is completely self-supporting. Canada Centre made an agreement with all the high schools in Galilee, which have accepted figure skating as a sport in their physical-education programs. They come twice a week to learn.

Israeli ice dancers Galit Chait and Sergei Sakhnovsky are the perfect example of the hybrid nature of skating in their country. Sakhnovsky was born in Moscow, but emigrated to Israel. Chait is Israeli-born. The pair competed in six international competitions while representing Israel, before competing at the world championship in Edmonton, where they finished twenty-third of thirty-three couples.

And Canada Centre has become a great meeting place, where Israeli Jews, Israeli Arabs, Orthodox Jews, United Nations peacekeepers, and generally an unusual mix of faiths and races skate and mix gleefully under one roof. Even people from Lebanon cross the border to "slip" across the ice. People instead of katoucha rockets. Laughter instead of terror.

Shmerkin was one new Israeli who heard the talk about Canada Centre. One day in 1991, Goldberg got a phone call from a new immigrant whose dream it was to represent Israel in international competition. Astonished, Goldberg said he wanted to see him skate first, and then they'd talk. It was Shmerkin, and he had no time to lose; he wanted to go to the 1992 Albertville Olympics. When Goldberg saw the five-foot-four-inch (160-centimeter) Shmerkin deliver skills the Metulla rink had never seen before, he was convinced. "I said, 'I will help you, although I don't know how we will find the money, but we will start in Canada Centre.'" At the time, Metulla had a rink that had opened only the year before Shmerkin appeared, but it was only one-third the size of an Olympic arena.

As it turned out, Shmerkin's Olympic dream had to wait another two years. Even though he automatically became an Israeli citizen when he immigrated to the country, the International Skating Union forbids a skater to represent a new country unless he or she had lived there at least a year. And at the time, "figure skating was zero" in Israel, Goldberg said. Israel became a provisional member of the ISU in 1992, and a full member only in 1994.

Currently, Israel has only four skating clubs, one in Metulla, one in Haifa, and one in and one near Tel Aviv. There are about one thousand figure skaters in the country, and half of them are in Metulla. Shmerkin currently trains in Oberstdorf, Germany, with Martin and Bruni Scotnicky, since there are no coaches in Israel yet who can guide an Olympic-level athlete. Shmerkin has finished eleventh at the past two world championships, his best finishes. In previous years, he has been hampered by illness, by the small rink, and by a lack of training time, missed while he was on army duty.

"His strength is his personality," said Bruni Scotnicky. "With all that is behind him in his life, he understands a lot of what's going on in this world. . . . He is very sensitive in his feelings. The problem is when he takes these things with him onto the ice. I try to make him as free as possible."

Shmerkin has been an inspiration to skating in Israel. "In Israel, children are very motivated to be the best," he said. Shmerkin helps them whenever he can. Once, he brought back fifteen pairs of skates from Europe, some purchased with his own money, to young Israeli skaters. After a Jewish community fund-raising campaign in Alberta in 1996, Shmerkin returned from the Edmonton world championship with fifty pairs of skates for Israel's youngsters.

With Shmerkin at the fore, Canada Centre offered the first Skate Israel international competition in the fall of 1995, attracting skaters from twenty-two countries. Unfortunately, three days before the event was to start, the northern part of Israel endured heavy shelling from Lebanon. "One hundred thousand people slept in shelters for a couple of nights," Steven Ain said. But there was no thought of canceling Skate Israel, the first international skating event in the Middle East. "They don't usually aim at Metulla," Ain said. "It's too small."

French pairs champions Sarah Abitbol and Stéphane Bernadis took home vivid memories of Skate Israel; they won a tough competition, defeating the promising Latvian pair of Elena Bereznaia and Oleg Shliakhov. "We heard the bombs," Bernadis said. "The army was everywhere. They play basketball [carrying] guns."

It was also an event to remember for Abitbol, who is of Jewish heritage. "For me, it was very good," she said. "My dream was to skate in Israel one day."

Soon there will be many more skaters in Israel, Shmerkin says, particularly if peace comes. These days, he skates to hear the "Hatikva," the Israeli national anthem. In Hebrew, it means hope.

"If the sun cannot bring peace to Israel," Shmerkin says, "maybe the ice can."

The World Junior Figure-Skating Championship

*F*or its first two years – 1976 and 1977 – this event was called the International Skating Union junior figure-skating championship. The competition wasn't that stiff, and Soviet skaters did not attend. But as soon as it was declared the world junior figure-skating championship in 1978, it became a popular event that served up the sport's future stars. In 1978, the Brian Boitano–Brian Orser rivalry was born. (They finished third and fourth, respectively.) Canadian pairs skaters Barbara Underhill and Paul Martini, together only six months, won a gold medal in this event in 1978, six years before they became world senior champions. Soviet Sergei Ponomarenko won gold in the ice-dancing event that year, too, but with a partner other than Marina Klimova, his future wife with whom he won Olympic gold in 1992. Since then, the world junior championships have given the world a peek at future stars like Paul Wylie, Kristi Yamaguchi, Rudy Galindo, and Todd Eldredge, all of the United States; 1992 Olympic champion Victor Petrenko; Yuka Sato of Japan; Surya Bonaly of France; and Russians Ekaterina Gordeeva and Sergei Grinkov. All were world junior champions.

Many of the stalwarts of professional skating ranks were world junior figure-skating champions: Paul Wylie of the United States (top left) in 1981, Yuka Sato of Japan (top right) in 1990, and Victor Petrenko of Ukraine (bottom right) in 1984. However, only Oksana Baiul of Ukraine (lower left) did not win the junior title. She did not even qualify for the event.

(Page 45) Jayson Dénommée is one of a handful of Canadian junior hopes. At eighteen, he became the Canadian junior silver medalist, and he finished third in a junior international "future stars" event at Skate Canada.

(Facing page) Barbara Underhill and Paul Martini

Kristi Yamaguchi was a precocious star, winning her junior singles skating world title in 1988, the same year she also won the world junior pairs title with Rudy Galindo in Brisbane, Australia. These early experiences led to her winning two senior world titles and an Olympic gold medal. Now she is one of the most respected and consistent of professional skaters.

Rudy Galindo, seventeen, and Kristi Yamaguchi, fifteen, as they finished third at the 1987 world junior event in Kitchener. Galindo won the men's title at this event by throwing in an unplanned triple Salchow. This was typical for Galindo. His coach, Jim Hulik, said that during practices in Kitchener, Galindo performed combinations with two triples "just to psyche everybody out. I guess he did the job." At the time, only three skaters at the senior level attempted back-to-back triples in combination.

All soft cheeks and long legs and bright eyes, the junior skaters of the world are a fast-moving lot. And, right now, particularly if they are Russian.

Young Russian men, women, pairs, and dancers dominated the world junior championship in Brisbane, Australia, in December 1995 in a way that made the rest of the bladed world gasp and wonder. With punch and flair and talent and depth, they swept the gold medals in all four disciplines. Yet, hadn't rinks in Russia closed down, turned into discos? Hadn't coaches left the country in droves for the United States, Canada, France, anywhere where there was hard currency and jobs? Hadn't the Russian skating federation scaled back its financial support to zilch, leaving the job to the clubs, many of them faltering and strapped for cash? Hadn't St. Petersburg skaters only two years before fled to Moscow, to Italy, to France, to train when ice conditions failed at home? Weren't their Zambonis all in a state of disrepair?

"The situation for sport is much harder for the young ones and the ones on the middle level," said Victor Kudryavtsev, the Russian coach of budding stars Ilia Kulik – a junior world champion only the previous year – and Maria Butyrskaia, the 1996 European bronze medalist. "For them, the parents must buy the costumes, and the lessons, and the equipment."

At least for Kulik, Kudryavtsev said, many things are free. "The government pays still, because he is on the national team." Still, Kudryavtsev, speaking in 1995, warned there was plenty of young talent still around, youth looking for a place to fly.

But not everybody believes the reports that the Russian gravy train has dried up completely. "They've been pulling our leg all along," said Canadian coach Louis Stong. "No coach, no ice, no money. You don't do the kind of things they've been doing without a darn strong junior program."

The most astonishing display at the world junior championship in Brisbane was that of the Russian women: they finished first, second, and third. The young women ranged in age from thirteen to sixteen years and were aggressive and fast, with all the tough tricks of their senior counterparts.

But there was a time not so long ago that Russian women couldn't find their way to a world podium. A few shone at the junior level over the years, but only two – Tatiana Andreeva in 1985 and Natalia Gorbenko in 1986 – won world junior championships. Neither made waves at the senior level. The first woman to go through the Soviet system and win a world or Olympic title was Oksana Baiul in 1993 – but by the time she did it, she represented the breakaway country of Ukraine.

When Baiul won the 1994 Olympic gold medal, women's skating in Russia was in such disarray that no Russian female singles skater competed at the Lillehammer Games. Their absence stemmed from an international edict intended to reduce the numbers of Olympic competitors. For the 1994 Olympics, the ISU accepted only those countries that made it to the final free-skating round of twenty-four skaters (for singles skaters) at the previous world championship in 1993 in Prague. Maria Butyrskaia was the only Russian female singles skater who attended that championship; when she finished only fifteenth in her qualifying round, and failed to advance to the event, much less the final free-skate, Russia lost its Olympic spot in that discipline altogether.

Russia was able to send only one woman to the 1993 world championship because, the previous year, its representative, Tatiana Rachkova, had failed to finish within the top ten. Unheralded and unknown, Rachkova, representing the Commonwealth of Independent States, had finished an unlucky thirteenth at the 1992 world championship in Oakland, California.

The Soviet Union could have sent two women to the 1992 world championship because of a top-ten finish the previous year at the event in Munich – with Yulia Vorobieva's tenth-place finish – while junior champion Natalia Gorbenko ended only nineteenth. But the void of talent was obviously deep and dark. Rachkova had no teammate at the 1992 event.

Yet, now that the Russian sport system is withering, the female skaters are beginning to skate circles around their peers. Irina Slutskaia, the 1995 world junior champion, became the first Russian woman to win the European championship in 1996 – just before she turned seventeen.

"Girls now skate well because they start to be free," said Alexei Mishin, the pensive Russian coach of Alexei Urmanov. "Before, they was suppressed. When they start to skate, and get good result, but then result go down a little bit, for example, because they were stuck in totalitarian system, [they would hear,] 'Why you skate not so good?' After that, they get a complex of 100 per cent."

Mishin suggested, "Now that they are free, they start to skate well. It affects girls [mentally] more than boys. With boys, nobody cares. They get good results in singles, and nobody was worried if somebody lost. But in the ladies, the system suppressed their skating.

"We had very good talent, but the talent was lost. There were many more talents, better than others who got to the top. The system was not correct."

At Brisbane, those times all seemed to be forgotten. The three Russian women, all wrapped in various hues of black and pink, were simply unbeatable, even without a Russian judge sitting on the panel. Sixteen-year-old Elena Ivanova, blonde, muscular, and powerful in the mold of 1981 world champion Denise Biellmann of Switzerland, won both the short and long program and, with absolute confidence, landed a triple Lutz–triple toe-loop combination, rarely seen even in the senior ranks. She also tossed in a second triple Lutz later in the program for good measure.

Brian Wells, at twenty-five, is a senior skater and too old to compete at world junior championships, but he reached into the junior ranks to find tiny Shelby Lyons, who had never skated pairs before. Wells is definitely from another generation. He finished sixth with his sister Ann-Marie at the world juniors in 1988 and 1989.

Elena Pingacheva moved from fourth to second overall after her stellar long-program performance, with five triples, including a triple Lutz, landed with no hesitation, no fear, and great speed.

Little Nadejda Kanaeva, only thirteen, actually finished in a tie with Pingacheva, but Pingacheva was awarded the silver medal because she finished ahead of Kanaeva in the long program. Some believe that the expressive Kanaeva may be the best of the three. Wearing a pink tutu, with suspenders and bows at her hips, Kanaeva, with her enormous blue eyes, looked like a little girl. But she did not skate like one. Performing to music from *West Side Story*, she landed a triple Lutz–double toe-loop combination, four other triples, and plenty of well-executed Biellmann-like spins.

Will Kanaeva fall by the wayside like many of her pressured predecessors? Perhaps not. She is trained by Elena Vodorezova, the first Soviet woman to win a world-championship medal – a bronze – in 1983 in Helsinki, Finland. Who could understand the drawbacks of an exacting results-oriented system better than she?

When the Russians were finished, many other young females of the world were left to ponder the future in their ice chips. Canada did not even send a skater to the event; twenty young women sought a berth in a special trial event, but the Canadian Figure Skating Association deemed that none were yet worthy. The United States currently has more hope; it has media darling Tara Lipinski, who, at age thirteen, won a berth to represent her country at the senior world championship with her bronze-medal win at the U.S. championship. She did not fare so well in Brisbane, finishing fifth, with a less ambitious program than she used at the U.S. championship. But before the Brisbane event was over, her coach, Jeff Di Gregorio, had packed his bags and left, their relationship severed over her loss. Lipinski headed to the school of Richard Callaghan, coach of Todd Eldredge.

The United States also has Shelby Lyons, a fourteen-year-old dark-eyed wonder, who qualified to go to the world senior championship in Edmonton as a pairs skater with Brian Wells with their effort at the U.S. nationals. Lyons finished eighth in Brisbane, but went on to win the 1996 U.S. junior women's title with a triple toe-loop–triple toe-loop combination, all the while amazing unflappable coach Kathy Casey. Casey watched in astonishment as Lyons learned all her triple jumps and became a pairs skater to boot, all within eighteen months.

Lyons and Wells also tried to become the first pairs skaters ever to land side-by-side triple loops at the U.S. championship in San Jose, California, in January 1996. Wells doubled his; Lyons landed hers perfectly. "I think when we hit the 1998 Olympics, Shelby is going to be right in there fighting for the top five [in the women's event]," Casey said of Lyons, who is all of seventy pounds (thirty-two kilograms) and stands four-foot-seven-inches (138 centimeters). "I don't think there's any stopping her."

Daniel Bellemare pushed the envelope and jumped to seniors.

France, a growing power in figure skating, has two or three promising young women, including Vanessa Gusmeroli, who, at age seventeen, finished sixth at the world juniors in Brisbane. But the country of bistros and chic design has an even-more-powerful backup of talented young men. "We have a fourteen-year-old boy [Vincent Restencourt] starting quads now in France," said French national coach Allen Schramm, a former American skater who was known for his artistic flair, footwork, and extraordinary body movement.

"And we have four or five boys from sixteen to eighteen who are very good," Schramm added. One of them is Stanick Jeanette, an eighteen-year-old fuzzy-chinned rebel, who had a chance to make the podium in Brisbane, but skated poorly. Jeanette, who finished second in a special junior men's event at Skate Canada in Saint John, New Brunswick, lets fly enormous triple-Axel combinations, but when he misses, at least in practice, he has been known to pound the ice and punch the air in anger and frustration.

At the world junior championship, male skaters could ill afford to make any mistakes. The top ten finishers all had triple Axels in their routines. And it took senior-level polish to win, too. Jumps alone did not help the boy from China. Sixteen-year-old Guo Zhengxin landed – perfectly – every jump in the book, even a triple Axel–triple toe-loop combination and a quadruple toe-loop, to finish third, but his presentation marks dropped markedly from 0.3 to 0.7 points from the level of his technical merit. Such drastic drops in the second mark have rarely been seen. The judges were giving an emphatic message about the importance of artistry.

The skater who had the spit and polish and the technical expertise was Alexei Yagudin of Russia, a fifteen-year-old training mate of 1994 Olympic champion Alexei Urmanov. And his well-rounded abilities led to some significant successes, despite his youth. Yagudin actually competed in the Centennial on Ice competition in St. Petersburg in February against some of the best seniors, and finished second, ahead of Urmanov.

"I have five skaters in my group," said Alexei Mishin, Yagudin's coach. "And they are nearly at the same level. Some days, one jumps better than Urmanov. They compete against each other."

One of Mishin's other pupils is Evgeny Pluschenko, an amazing thirteen-year-old, who finished sixth in Brisbane with an arsenal of all the triple jumps possible (although he did not complete the rotation of his triple Axel) and a level of showmanship that belies his years. Russia promises to be a power in the men's event for years to come.

Fortunately for Canada, there is hope in this area. Although Canada's best finish in Brisbane in the men's event was Daniel Bellemare's twenty-fourth placing, the fifteen-year-old Quebec skater is matching the skills of his young, restless peers. He landed his first triple Axel at age thirteen, and, even though he could have stayed at the junior level nationally another year, he stepped quickly up to senior and finished fifth behind Elvis Stojko. "I think Daniel could be one of the best," said coach Paul Wirtz, brother of Canadian pairs skater, Kris Wirtz. "He's got a good head. Nothing fazes him. He believes in himself. He's got an aggressive personality."

There are others, too. There is Canada's 1996 junior champion Collin Thompson, who has spent the past three years training in Lake Arrowhead, California, with Frank Carroll. He tried so many triple Axels in training

Stanick Jeanette,
rebel without a cause

within the past year that he developed "jumper's knee," a painful condition in which scar tissue forms around ruptured ligaments, and had to put them aside. There is Jayson Dénommée, an eighteen-year-old skater with a mature look and a triple Axel. And there is Ben Ferreira, a sixteen-year-old skater who landed a triple-Axel combination in the short program at the junior Canadian event – even though he did not start skating until he was almost twelve years old.

Canada won no medals at the world junior championship, although it sent ten skaters, but Russia continued its tradition of dominating pairs and dance competitions. Its winners in these two disciplines had to come from behind: pair Victoria Maksuta, fourteen, and Vladislav Zhovnirsky, seventeen, both tiny and childlike, dazzled judges with their perfect triple twists, throw triple Salchows, and throw double Axels. They overtook the Ukrainian team of Evgenia Filonenko, only thirteen, and Igor Marchenko, eighteen, who skated aggressively and swiftly, but took some major falls. Leading after the short program and third at the previous world junior championship, the Ukrainian pair looked stunned when their marks fluttered up and they won silver.

In ice dancing, Ekaterina Davydova and Roman Kostomarov of Russia took advantage of a last-minute fall by leaders Isabelle Delobel and Oliver Schoenfelder of France in the long program and moved from second to first overall. But with their speed, expert unison, and the quality of their steps and expression, the Russians probably didn't need the help.

How could this Russian dominance continue? In tough times, the Russians get tougher, Mishin explains. "In the time of communism, you take ten loaves and you eat two and refuse the rest," he says, eyes twinkling. "The dog with a full stomach never runs as strong."

The Professional World

*T*he professional world is wide and varied and year-round, encom-
passing shows on tiny ice surfaces at places such as Paramount
Canada's Wonderland, Florida's Sea World, or Atlantic City during
summer months. The Edmonton Opera Company even stepped into the fray
when it invited Toller Cranston to appear in Act Two of *Die Fledermaus* in
March, during the week of the world championship. Cranston performed on
skates on a special plastic ice surface, which also was trod upon by actors in
all manner of footwear. In addition, various tours, such as the Tom Collins
Tour of World Champions, offer plenty of work for titled pros, as does the
ten-year-old "Stars on Ice" tour that runs through nine cities in Canada and
fifty-five stops in the United States. The "Stars on Ice" tour, operated by International Management Group, a sport-management group, features a stellar
cast of world and Olympic champions, with Scott Hamilton at the forefront.

The wildly expansive world of professional skating during the 1995-96
season was all about transition: adapting, learning how to please under the
spotlights, moving on with life and opportunity.

Russians Marina Klimova and Sergei Ponomarenko remain as two of the most revered and successful ice dancers on the professional circuit with their riveting theme programs.

(Page 57) Scott Hamilton is known throughout the skating world as an unparalleled entertainer. In his unique routine to Hair, Hamilton traces the life of a hippie. On ice, he sheds his wig and transforms his funky vest and bell-bottoms into baby-boomer togs. He used this routine for the Sergei Grinkov tribute in Hartford, Connecticut, because he knew his friend would appreciate the humor.

(Facing page)
Nancy Kerrigan

Tonya Harding moved on, but not really. Aboard a yacht on the Williamette River in Oregon, she married machinist Michael Smith on December 23, 1995. Later, she scuffled with a family guest who sold a wedding photo for $100, mistakenly thinking that he had ruined a deal she had made to sell her own photos for $10,000. According to news reports, she rammed her car against the vehicle of her new relative. Four months later, Harding left the marriage, her second, his fourth. At one point, her new agent suggested Harding wanted to make an amateur comeback and have the United States Figure Skating Association lift her lifetime ban. No way, the USFSA responded quickly.

Nancy Kerrigan appeared to want to move on – right out of the skating spotlight. During the World Professional Championship in mid-December 1995, Kerrigan, a little heavier than when she won Olympic silver in 1994, stumbled and sprawled out of two moves that she used to make poetic: the camel spin and the spiral. She finished last of four competitors. She had married her agent, Jerry Solomon, in September 1995, and it was clear Kerrigan was yearning for a simpler life. It appears she may have it. The two-time Olympic medalist is expecting her first child in December 1996.

After twenty-three years of international competitions, 1980 Olympic champion Robin Cousins of Britain decided to trade in his skates for drama togs; he took his final competitive skating bow after the Challenge of Champions event in London, England, in December 1995. Skating to "Falling in Love with You Again," thirty-nine-year-old Cousins drew a standing ovation from a home crowd that had not seen him skate competitively since 1979 and from parents that had not seen him skate live in five years. Cousins will now turn his attention fully to choreography and theater work. For six months he toured England, bravely playing Frank N. Furter, the transvestite star of the *Rocky Horror Show*, resplendent in fishnet stockings and high heels. But he wanted, he said, to be taken seriously in the theater world, something he could not do when jumping back and forth from the footlights of the theater to the bright lights of skating. Still, skating holds a special place in his heart. "I only ever skated because I loved it," he said.

As Cousins was finding his way out of the professional world, Kurt Browning of Canada and Yuka Sato of Japan were pressing their way into it and dominating the results before season's end.

Sato's quick transition to the professional realm was made all the more remarkable by the fact that she had to travel halfway across the world to

Oksana Baiul has grown from a skinny waif with a skiff of blonde hair into a comely woman. Actually, she has grown five inches (thirteen centimeters) since winning the 1994 Olympic gold medal. Now eighteen, she lives in Connecticut, drives a Mercedes-Benz convertible, earns millions, and has an agent for the stars. She had greater success on tours than in competitions; she did not compete in the world professional championship nor the Challenge of Champions.

compete in events, sometimes enduring grinding jet lag. And although she emerged from a culture far different to that of the western world, she quickly and cleverly figured out what works in North American pro circles. With stunning, very versatile programs choreographed by Lea Ann Miller, a former U.S. pairs skater, and by Toller Cranston, Sato won four consecutive events against the best pro skaters the world had to offer: the Rider's Triple Crown Series in Boston, Massachusetts (defeating the powerful Denise Biellmann, Oksana Baiul, Elizabeth Manley – who at thirty was also having one of her

At thirty, Elizabeth Manley had one of her best competitive seasons. She earned a perfect mark of 6.0 at the Canadian professional championship in Hamilton – while running on only two hours' sleep. She skated to "The Impossible Dream," dedicating it to her friend, Ottawa sportscaster Brian Smith, who was shot and killed earlier in the season. She knelt down, kissed the ice, and earned a standing ovation.

best years – and Katarina Witt); the Canadian Professional Championship in Hamilton, Ontario (outskating Manley and Biellmann); the World Professional Championship in Landover, Maryland (defeating defending champion Kristi Yamaguchi, Biellmann, and Kerrigan); and the Challenge of Champions in London, England.

"My season started in April [1995], with a show in Japan," Sato said. "But it's different there. The shows are only on certain weekends every month. It gives me opportunity to come to North America."

Denise Biellmann, inventor of the famous spin, was always the skater to defeat in women's professional competitions. Her musical choices are unorthodox, and her style is muscular and athletic. Well known as a fitness buff who also pursues yoga, the thirty-four-year-old Swiss skater has developed a fitness line in Europe, including a weight machine, aerobics clothing, and health and fitness food. She aims to become the Jane Fonda of Europe.

Kurt Browning finally found his step in the professional world. "I'm feeling more like an entertainer now," he said. "I'm really comfortable with that feeling and that freedom, and I'm not held so accountable anymore for my performance, because I know what I can do, especially when I'm happy. I can give people what they want, which is not necessarily the triple toe-loop after the triple Axel. I love that, because I always thought that's what my strength was."

Brian Boitano in full flight in his long professional career. Among other events, the 1988 Olympic champion won the Gold Championship in Vancouver. But he also became a choreographer and director in a made-for-television skating special called "Skating Romance" because he was not happy with the direction skating was headed: aimed at a funky, younger audience. Boitano wanted to bring it back to female viewers – who had created much of its popularity in the first place.

Kurt Browning married National Ballet of Canada dancer Sonja Rodriguez on June 30, 1996, at the Royal Canadian Yacht Club in Toronto. He had proposed to her at a "Stars on Ice" stop in Toronto the year before in front of thousands of spectators. However, because of their schedules, they saw each other only twice in the following five weeks. "Thanks to Bell Mobility, we bought the ring together," Browning said.

But the choice also makes for a harried schedule. During one week in November, Sato skated twice in the United States, did a show in Japan, flew back to do the Boston competition, and returned to Japan the next day. "The day after, I had a show in north Japan," she said. "This was tough. It took twenty-four hours of flying, and I had to be on the ice the next day – and there was a twelve-hour time difference.

"I try to be really tough, but sometimes I can't." Sato, the 1994 world (amateur) champion, missed one other competition, the Ultimate Four event in Boston in December, because of illness.

Kurt Browning has less ground to cover, flying from his base in Toronto to various events in North America, but, after a disastrous first season, the four-time world champion also finally found his feet as a professional during the 1995-96 season – even defeating perennial pro king Brian Boitano at the World Professional Championship. "This year has been totally different," Browning said. "Last year was my first day of school in a new town."

At the beginning of his pro career, Browning got off on the wrong foot – literally; his skates stubbornly refused to break in, and, when he performed at the Canadian Pro Championships in 1994, he had to skate without the top hook done up – or he couldn't skate at all. He had also just recovered from a shoulder injury that sidelined him for six weeks. "And I didn't actually recover very well from the Olympics [in which he finished only sixth]," he said. "I was still dealing with a bunch of leftover feelings from that. I was just not a happy boy.

"I really wasn't ready to compete at that level, but I stepped on the ice and I tried. And I tried to do jumps I hadn't done in practice for three weeks. It was really bad management on my part. But I learned the hard way. Scott Hamilton said, 'Welcome to the club.'"

Gradually, the shoulder healed, and Browning, who had developed severe back problems before the 1992 Albertville Games, got back in shape, both physically and mentally, helped by a personal trainer and fortified by his engagement to Sonja Rodriguez, a dancer with the National Ballet of Canada. (They married in June 1996 in Toronto.) "It's been fun again," he said.

In spite of his lackluster first season, Browning found himself busier than ever in the second. From October 20 to December 16, he had only four days off. He won the Starlight Challenge in New York, and after he won the Canadian Professional Championship in December 1995, with programs he had run through only four or five times, he said, "My goal at Landover [at the World Professional Championship] is just to scare Boitano."

He did more than that. Although Boitano won the technical program with his powerful jumps, Browning overtook him in the artistic test with his rubber-legged performance to the Commodores' 1970 hit "Brick House." "It means a lot to me because I had a waterlogged year last year and couldn't get going," he told a reporter. "I really kind of saw a night like this not happening again. Having a year like that means you don't take skating for granted."

Boitano had won the event six times previously.

Yuka Sato, a professional gold mine

Maia Usova and Alexander Zhulin were supposed to reinstate as amateurs for the 1995-96 season. However, a groin injury that Zhulin suffered during the Tour of World Champions in 1995 scuttled that idea. As soon as they participated in the Northwestern Mutual Life Team Championship in Milwaukee, they lost their eligible status for the last time. Their life situations also dictate their future. Separated as husband and wife, they can no longer work the five to six hours a day needed to compete as amateurs. While Usova lives in Lake Placid, New York, Zhulin now lives in Simsbury, Connecticut.

Browning went on to win the Ultimate Four event, taking advantage of a bizarre set-up in the new open event in which four skaters had to qualify in a short program for a championship round (with two skaters) and a consolation round (with two skaters.) Browning, skating poorly, defeated Philippe Candeloro of France, who skated even worse. Paul Wylie of the United States skated best of all, and attracted the top marks, but, because he did so in the consolation round, could finish no higher than third. Scott Hamilton, battling the flu, finished last, and impishly flouted the amateur-based rules by landing an illegal back flip.

Flouting and forgetting the rules seemed to be the order of the day in the open competitions. At the Ultimate Four, skaters were limited to four triple jumps. Surya Bonaly wildly exceeded that number – although she had been doing only four in practice – and finished second to Chen Lu. Kristi Yamaguchi skated an uncharacteristically poor short program with major mistakes, missed the championship round, then skated best of all in the final. But knowing she could finish no higher than third and no worse than third (Yuka Sato had withdrawn, leaving only three women in the event), Yamaguchi did five triples.

The Starlight Challenge at the outdoor Wollman Rink in New York City's Central Park was even a more chaotic open competition. The women were allowed only three jumps in the long program, but rules were ignored blatantly. Nicole Bobek tried four, fell three times, but won first place and $50,000 (U.S.). Rosalynn Sumners landed two double Axels, while only one was allowed, attempted no triples, and used vocal music, which is not permitted. She finished third of three entries and won $30,000.

Confusing? "All of these events are feeling their way, and everybody is making mistakes," American coach Kathy Casey says. "Everyone, the whole skating world, is learning from them, the coaches, the skaters, and the promoters. I think in the end it will sort itself out and be positive for our sport."

A *Tribute to Sergei Grinkov*

*T*he death of Sergei Grinkov during the 1995-96 season left a wound that may never quite heal in the hearts of his family and friends, in amateur and professional skaters, in skating fans, and even in that part of the world that knows little about split twists and Salchow throws. All were touched; all recognized the loss of perfection and love in the loss of one so young and so full of life.

They were like two flowers stuck together, Marina Zoueva thought when she first saw them in 1982 in Moscow – a tiny eleven-year-old girl named Ekaterina Gordeeva and a skinny fifteen-year-old teen named Sergei Grinkov, who had just been matched together as pairs skaters.

"How do you say it in Canada? Cute?" said the Russian-born choreographer. "They were cute."

The previous year, Grinkov had competed as a singles skater in Budapest, Hungary, with three triples, but he was a reluctant participant in the pairs match-up. "He said, 'I never can lift them [meaning girls],'" recalled Zoueva, whose life and career has been inextricably intertwined with the pair known as G and G. "He was not so strong."

The on-ice performances of Ekaterina Gordeeva and Sergei Grinkov were reflections of their off-ice lives, said friend Brian Orser. "It was like something out of a fairy tale. With me, whenever I was trying to put together a benefit show, they were always the first to say yes. I put together two 'Skate the Dream's [to raise money for AIDS research], and they came. They knew no one was getting paid, but they didn't care about that. They were just happy to be there. Once, they couldn't do a show in Calgary because their skating federation wouldn't allow them to come. Katya phoned me personally and promised she'd come to the next 'Skate the Dream.'"

(Facing page)
Gordeeva, now skating solo

Ekaterina Gordeeva and Sergei Grinkov in the spring of 1984 as they were helping their choreographer, Marina Zoueva, get her arts degree. The newly paired couple demonstrated her choreography. Zoueva passed with flying colours. In the left insert are G & G, as they were affectionately called, as they looked skating in 1985 in the Soviet Union; right insert, as they appeared in 1986.

Ekaterina Gordeeva and Sergei Grinkov at the 1987 world championship in Cincinnati. "Sergei loved to eat," said Brian Orser, who befriended the couple on a world tour in 1986. "Quite often on tour, when you wanted to go for dinner, they were one of the first to call. He didn't like turkey, but he liked sushi, and so did Katya. He'd eat his, and finish hers, too."

Two weeks later, the young skaters were split up, but already a bond had been formed; in spite of what the coaches said, little Gordeeva and Grinkov wanted to stay together. And so they did. Into Zoueva's group they eventually came, thankfully as a unit, and under her wing they grew into the most revered of pairs skaters, ethereal in their movements, unerring in their unison, glowing with a purity of edge and a quality of love others could only dream about.

Later in life, they learned they never wanted to be apart, both on and off the ice, but it was not to be. On November 20, 1995, Sergei Grinkov died of a massive heart attack at the age of twenty-eight, while practicing for a "Stars on Ice" tour in Lake Placid, New York. He left behind his Katya (the diminutive of Ekaterina), who had become his wife four years earlier, and their three-year-old daughter, Daria (affectionately called Dasha), the pride of Grinkov's heart.

At the 1989 world
championship in
Paris. "Sergei was
very sweet," said
Kurt Browning, who
skated with the
Russian pair on
"Stars on Ice" tours.
"Once he devoted
himself to Katya, he
had the impression
that other people
should do the same.
So if you were flirting
too much [with
Katya], he'd always
sort of frown at you,
like a grandfather
would. He was
very traditionalist
that way."

(Insert) At the 1989 world championship in Paris. (Right) At the 1990 world championship in Halifax. "What sticks in my mind the most about [Gordeeva and Grinkov] was how humble they were," said "Stars on Ice" choreographer Sandra Bezic. "They never made any demands. They were always so thankful for everything. They always thought they were lucky to be in 'Stars on Ice.' I'd look at them and say we are the ones that are thankful that you are with us."

They were Russians living in the United States, and Grinkov, on the surface quiet and reserved, had just been stumbling his way into the English language. But Americans wept at his passing. So did other nations, touched by the couple who seemed so remotely perfect, yet were dear to their hearts. All were warmed by their absolute love, their obvious respect for each other.

"Sergei was a very proud person," said Zoueva, who now works and lives in Ottawa, Ontario. "He wanted his life, everything, to be perfect. Their skating was so clean. He never missed a single element in his program, except at the [Lillehammer] Olympics. He had a perfect sport life, a perfect life. He had the perfect wife. And they had perfect baby."

So perfect that in her choreography Zoueva was inspired to use the theatrical Rachmaninov to depict her pair as Rodin sculptures for a professional program. "Sergei's body was like a Greek god's. And her body is just like a sculpture," Zoueva said. "You can't add anything to them. You just take what they have and fix [the moment]. This moment, how people love each other, is perfect. I wanted to fix this moment for Sergei and Katya forever, how they love each other."

But perfection doesn't always last, as flowers don't, and Gordeeva knew it. In the fall of 1995, Gordeeva took a special interest in a skating friend who had lost her husband to cancer just six months before and was left with a two-month-old baby boy. Gordeeva told her, "Sometimes when you have everything so perfect in life, God just takes something away from you." Two days later, Grinkov died.

Their skating family was left in shock. Gordeeva remained strong, at least at first. "The day Sergei died, the whole ['Stars on Ice'] company came over to her condo, just to be there," said Canadian skating star Brian Orser, who befriended the pair after first touring with them as amateurs in 1986. (Gordeeva and Grinkov once spent Christmas with Orser's parents in Florida.) "They were all crying. She said, 'Please tell them to stop crying. I'll be fine.' But in Moscow [at Grinkov's funeral], you could see the strain on her face."

"It is a Russian tradition that the partner that is left must be the strongest in the room, because the other is watching," explained International Management Group (IMG) agent Kevin Albrecht, whose young son often played with Daria on the Zambonis at the rinks. (Gordeeva and Grinkov were clients of IMG, which manages skaters and events.) "Many people thought she was just in shock, but she was the strong one."

Sergei and Katya with choreographer Marina Zoueva in their 1994 Olympic costumes, dressed like padres

But later, during her forty-day mourning period in Moscow, Gordeeva dissolved into tears, in despair over her loss.

To outsiders and even to some other skaters, Grinkov had walked tall and silent, like a soft, giant shadow behind the shining face of his Katya, whose command of the English language came earlier and much more easily. Always, Gordeeva did the talking, while Grinkov hovered quietly nearby. But those who knew him best saw a different side of him.

"When I would walk past the dressing room and other Russians were visiting, they were always laughing hysterically and joking, really loud laughter," said Kurt Browning. "I thought, wow, he seemed so quiet. But in his own language, he wasn't quiet at all. He was hilarious. He was a really big, sweet, strong man. It really, really hurt when he died."

"One of the things I remember most about Sergei was his grin," said Sandra Bezic, who choreographed a "Stars on Ice" number for the pair, appropriately enough to "The Man I Love" by Ella Fitzgerald. "Sometimes he wouldn't pay attention to some steps I was showing, and I'd go up to him and say, 'You didn't hear a damn thing I said, did you?' And he'd say no, and I'd show him the steps, and we'd laugh.

"He took his skating very seriously, but he didn't take himself seriously. And his grin is Dasha's grin. Exactly the same. It's a mischievous grin. He had a twinkle in his eyes. He was a devil in his own quiet way. He always looked like the Cheshire cat."

Marina Zoueva knows the grin better than most: she finds it astonishing that Daria's smile and her eyes are so like Grinkov's, particularly when he was her age. Even their laughter is strangely alike, bright and happy, Zoueva says. When Gordeeva looks at her daughter, she sees her husband.

Perhaps Grinkov inherited his lopsided grin from his father, a police officer in Moscow, then passed it like a torch to Daria. Both of Grinkov's parents were officers in the force. "Sergei was more like his father," Zoueva said. "I never saw his father without a smile. He always looked like a strong man. He looked very healthy. It was a shock for the family when he died." Grinkov's father died of a heart attack in his fifties, about six years before his son died the same way.

Grinkov never showed his pain, his stress, his emotions – but more and more, especially after the birth of Daria, he showed his light heart to the world. The Grinkov twinkle was perhaps one of the factors that appealed to American star Scott Hamilton, who took the pair under his wing when they

Skating to Bach's "Moonlight Sonata" at the 1994 Olympics

As a choreographer for "Stars on Ice," Sandra Bezic had the task of designing a program for Gordeeva and Grinkov in the fall of 1994. She chose "The Man I Love" by Ella Fitzgerald. "I wanted to capture what I watched on a daily basis and the way they looked at each other," she said. "Like lovers stealing kisses in a park. It was a very simple number. I didn't want choreography to get in the way of the relationship. It was the quintessential love song."

arrived in North America as professional skaters in 1991. At the time, Hamilton, who calls himself the Grinkovs' "self-appointed godfather," was producer of "Stars on Ice," and, when they joined it, he gave them things to do that were fun, he said.

"When you look at Sergei's presence and his physical size, it's deceiving, because there was a gentleness and always a wonderful sense of humor and an instant ability to laugh, and I like that in people," Hamilton said. "They were an easy audience to my sick sense of humor."

The Hamilton–Grinkov friendship was based on fun and laughter. The friends from two different worlds and cultures first met during the mid-1980s in a rink in Europe that Hamilton can no longer place. But he does remember the scene with clarity. "I was in Europe [commentating] for CBS and sat at the end of the boards, watching practice, when I noticed this little girl," he said, recalling his first sight of Gordeeva. "She was running the practice, and she had this giant, tall, skinny partner, and she was this tiny, skinny, short thing, and she was saying, 'We're going to do this. We're going to do that.' She was doing all the talking, and her partner could barely keep up with her. She was definitely very focused and very into this practice and getting the whole thing done. I was completely blown away. . . . I was an instant fan."

Together in St. Petersburg, Russia

Over the years, the Grinkovs and Hamilton slowly built up an enduring friendship, and, eventually, Hamilton and Grinkov developed a goofy, back-and-forth, one-upmanship routine that made words seem unimportant. "I'd get him three or four times a day," Hamilton said. "He'd look at me sometimes as if to say, 'What are you going to do next?'"

One of Hamilton's favorite photographs, taken during rehearsals last year, shows the unlikely twosome – giant, dark Grinkov and short, balding Hamilton – sitting atop the rink boards, mimicking two rock stars playing base guitars. "One of his cheeks is full of air, going boom-ba-boom-boom," Hamilton said, laughing.

Their friendship spilled over into routines they did together for "Stars on Ice." It started with Hamilton, who was to dance with Gordeeva for two minutes before the Russian pair did a solo performance. All the while, Grinkov would watch Hamilton intently. Later, during a group routine in the show, Hamilton would cheekily repeat the maneuver, only to find Grinkov tapping him on the shoulder.

"I brush him off, like 'Don't bother me, I'm busy,'" Hamilton said. "And he hits me harder. I turn around to look, and my nose goes into his chest and I

The happy family. Sergei holds daughter Daria in one arm, Katya in the other. On the far left is Fedor Andreev, the son of choreographer Marina Zoueva, who was born the year the Russian pair were matched together in Moscow.

realize I'm up against something a little more powerful than what I want to deal with, and I tiptoe away." It became a regular part of the tour routine.

"The first time [Grinkov] tapped me on the shoulder, he said, 'That's my wife' in English – and he didn't like to speak English a lot," Hamilton said.

In spite of the language barriers, Hamilton knew they were communicating extremely well when Grinkov had to explain one of Hamilton's jokes to Gordeeva.

As Grinkov learned more English, and after Daria's birth, his face during performances became more open; the warm soul shone through, so that audiences could see what his close friends saw every day. "The better his English got, the bigger his personality got," Kurt Browning said.

"In the beginning, you would just get a nod from him," Brian Orser said. "Then it got to 'Hello, Brian' in his accent. He would chuckle trying to say that."

Browning was astonished while training in Lake Placid in November 1995 to hear Grinkov string together English sentences in a friendly greeting. "He was coming to the rink and saying, 'Good morning, Kurt. And how are you?' And I'd say, 'Oh hi, Sergei. I'm good. And you?' He'd always say, 'Oh, I'm not too bad.' We [members of the tour] didn't really realize all [his] little Sergei-isms until we all started saying them to each other. When we'd want to remember him, we'd all say, 'Ab-so-lute-ly!' It was his favorite word.

The Grinkovs were known, in their early days, as unusual in that they were pairs skaters who could do quadruple twists. They did only two or three in their competitive career. (Right) As professional skaters, their twist moves were easy, high, and light. Gordeeva has so much time and confidence in the air that she has raised her arms above her head. Always, the couple looked at each other on the ice.

"We were on the tour for fifty dates together, with catering at the rink, and Scott would say to him every other show, 'Ready for free food, Sergei?' He'd reply, 'Ab-so-LUTE-ly!'"

Sandra Bezic, while working with Gordeeva and Grinkov on "Stars on Ice" tours, admitted that, because of the language barrier, she never really knew quite what Grinkov was thinking. He rarely spoke, although he understood everything, she said.

"They were just so special to have around," she said. "It's not something that we're just all saying now. We said it on a daily basis, 'Look at that! Look at them!' I think they really valued what they were and what they had.

"He was a rock. Not much could shake him. He would get frustrated when he was working, like anybody would. But he never showed it that much. Maybe to Katya. But he was a very elegant man, a very private man."

It was no secret, however, how much love he had for Katya, and for Daria, whom he spoiled and "totally adored," according to Bezic. On the last day of Grinkov's life, Hamilton jokingly cried out to him during practice, "Tomorrow is a Dasha day!" – meaning that Daria was to come for a visit from Connecticut, where she had been staying with Gordeeva's mother at their home in Simsbury. Grinkov's reply was to throw his arms jubilantly into the air. But he never saw his Dasha again.

He loved all children, Marina Zoueva said. His older sister, Natalia, a cosmetician in Moscow, has two daughters, with whom Grinkov often happily played. And Zoueva's own son, Fedor Andreev, was special to him. Fedor was born the year that Gordeeva and Grinkov were matched up together. "I have known him since I was born," said Fedor, who was thirteen when Grinkov died.

Fedor did not take up skating until his family moved to Canada about five years ago; and it was Grinkov who nudged him into the sport. Grinkov gave him plenty of advice, both on skating and on life. He told Fedor, "If you start something, always try to excel, or don't even start at all. Never try to save your energy in the warm-up if you want to have a good result. Don't whine before practice, because the practice won't get any shorter." With all of this in mind, Fedor finished second in the free-skate in the novice men's event at the 1996 Canadian championship in Ottawa, and fourth overall.

Fedor acknowledged Grinkov's faith in him by skating in the "Stars on Ice" tribute in Hartford, Connecticut, on February 27, 1996. He was the youngest performer in the group, skating to a sold-out rink. "It meant a lot to

Grinkov, waving to a "Stars on Ice" crowd in Toronto

me, because I knew I was doing something good, skating for Sergei," Fedor said. "And hoping he'd see what everyone was doing for him, and that we all love him very much and miss him a lot."

Fedor didn't forget Grinkov, and Grinkov never forgot him. In March 1995, Fedor had been astonished to find that Grinkov, who had been busy on tour, had taken the time to send him a birthday present through the mail: a pair of in-line skates. "They are amazing," he said. "It was just unexpected. I was really excited, because it was my first pair of rollerblades."

Fedor last saw Grinkov in the month before he died, when the famous pair visited Ottawa. "As usual, we went to Pizza Hut," the budding skater said, tracing the visit's highlights in his own mind. "Sergei was always laughing. We had a good time."

Grinkov's friends and family are left with full memories. In Fedor's closet hangs the outfit Grinkov wore during the short program at the 1989 world championship in Paris, which he and Gordeeva won, oblivious to the tragedy that lay ahead. It is elegant and black and a gift to Fedor from Gordeeva. It was her favorite.

"I haven't grown into it yet," Fedor said.

It may take a while, indeed.

*T*he *United States Figure-Skating Championship*

*I*n 1914, American skating pioneers George Browne and Irving Brokaw created the first International Figure Skating Championships of America – for all four skating disciplines – mainly to promote the flamboyant international skating style of Jackson Haines. The event was, in effect, the first U.S. championship, but the association between Canadian and American skaters was so close that Canadian Norman Scott won the first men's title. Since the United States Figure Skating Association (USFSA) was first formed in 1921, it has grown into one of the largest skating associations in the world, and now sports about 120,000 members. The 1996 U.S. championship was held in San Jose, California, from January 8 to 14, about a month before the Canadian championship.

Rudy Galindo.

Without Galindo, the national championship in San Jose might have been merely a show of the sort of power that the United States is mounting in the sport of toe picks and triples in almost every discipline. With Galindo, the event became an affair of the heart, to be treasured always. For Galindo, the forgotten skater, made a large crowd weep and chant and cheer.

Rudy Galindo was terrified at living up to expectations during his qualifying round at the world figure-skating championship in Edmonton. "I felt really dizzy," he said. "I felt like I wanted to pass out. I felt my insides tighten up." Nevertheless, Galindo won the qualifer.

(Page 87) Renee Roca and Gorsha Sur, a hybrid of American and Soviet skating programs, skated to "House of the Rising Sun" as their free-dance because they were tired of hearing a spate of Latin programs in ice dancing. "I knew this song in Russia," said Sur. "Everything comes ten years later to Russia, so when I was growing up, I heard it." The couple had only five weeks to work on the program before the U.S. championship, in which they finished second.

Within less than a week, Galindo went from being a trailer-park resident with a desperately unlucky life to being the recipient of a six-figure contract to skate in the lucrative Tom Collins Tour of World Champions. That's what winning the U.S. championship of hearts did for the twenty-six-year-old Mexican-American, who hadn't competed in an international competition for two years; who had lost his coach, Jim Hulik, the man who had guided him to win the 1987 world junior championship, to colon cancer in late 1989; who had lost his father, Jess, to a heart attack in April 1993; who had lost his thirty-four-year-old brother, George, to AIDS that same year; who had lost another coach, Rick Inglesi, also to AIDS, in 1995; who had lost his pairs partner, Kristi Yamaguchi, and had watched her career soar while his turned to cinders; and who, with no training funds forthcoming from the USFSA, had had to take six months off training to earn money coaching children. "I did everything myself," said Galindo, now coached by his sister Laura. "I put money away." Galindo says he skates to forget.

He was an unlikely contender, everybody figured, when he showed up for the championship in his home town of San Jose. It was his last chance. He figured he would turn professional if he failed to finish in the top six. (His best finish as a singles skater at a national championship was the fifth he earned in 1993. He twice won the U.S. title as a pairs skater with Yamaguchi, won a world junior title with her, and even finished fifth at the senior world championship in 1990 in Halifax, Nova Scotia, as a pairs skater.) On top of everything else, he had suffered from asthmatic bronchitis at the past two U.S. championships. Two weeks before the San Jose event, he became so ill that he had to take antibiotics. How could anyone even consider him a contender?

But Galindo always had prodigious talent, from the time he was a junior skater and would throw extra triples into a program at will. The night of his long-program performance in San Jose was pure magic. Even during the warm-up, Galindo landed an unerring series of triple-triple combinations; he had trained himself to stick a triple toe-loop onto the end of any triple he did. Had anyone in history ever had such a warm-up?

Galindo skated last; a script could not have been written with more impact. During the program, the crowd erupted noisily every time he landed a jump. Twenty seconds before he finished, the crowd was on its feet, applauding, and did not sit down again, even after Galindo jubilantly left the ice. They chanted for perfect sixes. Galindo got two, for his presentation to the music of *Swan Lake*. "Roo-dy! Roo-dy! Roo-dy!" they chanted. When

Ignoring distraction was the key to Galindo's success.

Galindo's name popped up on the screen at center ice – in first place – the crowd's screams echoed off the rafters. Almost astonishingly, Galindo dethroned heavy favorite, Todd Eldredge, who had already won three U.S. titles and was the defending world silver medalist. It was one of the greatest performances in skating history, a wild, victorious, flawless, unexpected point in time.

"I can't describe this moment," said Galindo, who admitted he had earlier visualized himself on the ice and "the crowd standing for some reason.

"My jumps seemed so light and easy. I didn't have to try so hard at all."

The victory, he said, was sweeter than the two U.S. pairs gold medals he won, "because I did it on my own."

Todd Eldredge, stunned in a surprising loss

The women's event was another story. All was not well with Nicole Bobek, who had earned the United States three berths for the 1996 world championship by winning the bronze medal at the world event in Birmingham, England, the previous year. But American officials were clearly unimpressed that Bobek did not take the time to heal an ankle injury when she accepted $90,000 (U.S.) to skate in the twenty-city "Nutcracker on Ice" tour the month before the U.S. championship in January. When she had to withdraw from the U.S. championship after finishing third in the short program, the world international committee, headed by judge James Disbrow, refused to give Bobek a medical bye to the world championship – even though orthopedist Dr. Warren King said there was a painful inflammation to the inside of her ankle that would not allow her to continue. Bobek said the injury was so painful, and her ankle so swollen, she could not sleep. "It's quite swollen and very tender," the doctor confirmed.

The committee was tight-lipped about its decision to exclude Bobek and send winner Michelle Kwan, silver medalist Tonia Kwiatkowski, and thirteen-year-old bronze medalist Tara Lipinski to the world championship. Had Bobek been given the medical bye, Lipinski would have been bumped from the world team, despite her medal finish. When asked how Bobek's situation differed from those of Todd Eldredge and Nancy Kerrigan, both of whom had received medical byes in the past, Disbrow would not elaborate, saying only that "the team, is best represented by these three" and that the committee did not look at precedents. When the media questions persisted, the news conference was abruptly ended. Disbrow's terse answers prompted a flurry of newspaper articles that railed against the decision. "BOBEK ICED – BIG TIME," stated a headline in the *San Jose Mercury News*. "Just when you think maybe

Nicole Bobek, the unpredictable. After Detroit coach Richard Callaghan had steered her to a U.S. title and a world bronze medal in 1995, Bobek left him in mid-December for Barbara Roles Williams, her ninth coach in twelve years. "I didn't feel like things were working as well as last year," she said. "I had to find the right training atmosphere." As an afterthought, Bobek said, "There are probably still one hundred coaches I haven't been through."

figure skating isn't so corrupt after all . . . the sport manages to screw up its image. Nicole Bobek was jobbed Saturday night. Big time," the article read.

Still, Lipinski won her spot on the team by landing six triples, an awesome feat for one so young, and a sign of the strength that the United States is gaining in figure skating. Amber Corwin, who finished sixth, showed off a triple toe-loop–triple toe-loop combination, and Sidne Vogel, a native of Alaska, who finished fourth, also showed enormous potential among the women.

The United States is also knee-deep in talented, risk-taking men. Daniel Hollander, who won the bronze medal, couldn't do triple jumps six years ago and had to battle a problem of self-doubt. But the martial-arts aficionado, who trains in Detroit, showed a comedic personality on the ice, along with exceedingly difficult spin combinations. And he also tried a tremendously difficult triple Axel–triple loop combination that no other male in the world attempted.

And there was more. Of seventeen men who competed in the senior men's event, all but four tried triple-Axel combinations in the short program. Galindo was the only one to do a triple Axel–triple toe-loop, but among the rest, Todd Eldredge, Trifun Zivanovic (in only his first year as a senior), two-time U.S. champion Scott Davis, and John Baldwin, Jr., all landed triple-doubles well. Others came very close. Indeed, there is power to spare in the United States.

And from New York to Los Angeles, there are promising pairs skaters. The 1995 world bronze medalists, Jenni Meno and Todd Sand, won their third U.S. title, but not very easily. Kyoka Ina and Jason Dungjen almost pulled off an upset by defeating them in the short program when they successfully landed triple toe-loops (Sand fell on his attempt), and then receiving a set of controversial marks that placed them second after the long program. Meno and Sand, lyrical in the vein of Ekaterina Gordeeva and Sergei Grinkov, their idols, lack the technical prowess that the ambitious Ina and Dungjen show.

Wonderkid Shelby Lyons and her partner, Brian Wells – who traveled nine thousand miles (14,000 kilometers) across the United States in his less-than-able car to find a pairs partner – finished third, with a cluster of difficult elements and jumps. But even the fourth-place team, Stephanie Stiegler and John Zimmerman IV, together only seven months, are an arresting pair. Zimmerman is powerful and strong – he does a one-arm overhead lift that is awe-inspiring – but the fast, dynamic pair, coached by 1988 Olympic bronze medalist Peter Oppegard, depended only on double jumps – as yet. They will bear watching in the future.

The dance event became a struggle between reigning champions Renee Roca and Gorsha Sur and a married couple, Elizabeth Punsalan and Jerod Swallow, who were U.S. champions before Roca and Sur reinstated as eligible skaters in 1992. The tension between the two couples has been palpable; Roca and Sur acted as Punsalan and Swallow's choreographers before they reinstated, and when Sur, who defected from the former Soviet Union in 1990, hurriedly sought American citizenship so that he and Roca could represent the United States at the 1994 Olympics, Punsalan and Swallow signed a petition urging that the request not be fast-tracked.

Scott Davis faced a barrage of questions at the U.S. championship about his vertigo before Skate Canada.

Jenni Meno and Todd Sand married in her hometown of Cleveland, Ohio, on July 22, 1995, spent their honeymoon in Maui, and then proceeded to win their third U.S. title in San Jose, California, and their second consecutive world bronze medal in pairs in Edmonton. They are known for their lyrically romantic performances, in the vein of Ekaterina Gordeeva and Sergei Grinkov, their skating heros.

This time, Punsalan and Swallow, vastly improved under the guidance of another Russian immigrant, Igor Shpilband, won all sections of the competition, except for the second compulsory dance. During a news conference, Swallow appeared to bend over backward to heal the rift; he constantly thanked Roca and Sur for allowing the United States two berths at the world championship in Edmonton by finishing in the top ten at the previous world championship. Roca and Sur said the issue was "not a problem."

"I think the personal stuff should be left to further discussions," Sur said.

After finishing second, Roca and Sur had 1984 Olympic champion Christopher Dean redesign their original dance, the *paso doble*, five weeks before the world championship. They still finished only fourteenth in Edmonton, four spots lower than their previous appearance, while Punsalan and Swallow, with their fast, dramatic programs, finished an impressive seventh.

U.S. silver medalists Kyoka Ina and Jason Dungjen (top) came close to winning the national championship with solid performances, while the new partnership of Stephanie Stiegler and John Zimmerman (bottom) was brilliant in finishing fourth. Tokyo-born Ina and the veteran Dungjen took pains in getting to know each other during the season, particularly during a stint training in Canada. Zimmerman was close to quitting before he hooked up with Stiegler, only seven and a half months before U.S. nationals. "We started right away with work that was a couple of shoe sizes too big," said coach Peter Oppegard, a former Olympian.

U.S. dance champions Elizabeth Punsalan and Jerod Swallow, married in 1993, got their 1995-96 season off to a slow start because of injury. Swallow felt such pain in his groin area during October 1995 that some thought he had appendicitis, but really he had inflamed muscles caused by a muscle imbalance in a hip and aggravated by choreography that called for repetitive leg motions in one direction. The couple missed international competitions in France and Japan. They did not start training again until December 1, only about six weeks before the U.S. championship. Still, they won.

Only one year out of the junior ranks, Eve Chalom and Mathew Gates were surprising bronze medalists. Gates is still a British citizen, although he has been training in Detroit for four years.

Joining the race at home were surprise bronze medalists Eve Chalom and Mathew Gates, who had been junior champions the previous year. Gates, who was born in England, said they expected to finish within the top ten and hoped for seventh. Their fast rise to the top is even more remarkable because Chalom wears a hearing aid in a discipline in which response to the music and its rhythms is crucial. Chalom was born with a 50-per-cent hearing loss in her right ear, but became completely deaf for six months at age four after she was struck by a car while riding on the back of a bicycle. Her hearing returned gradually, but currently doctors are monitoring her condition. Alarmed by a recent deterioration of her hearing, Chalom has learned to read lips and use sign language.

Chalom and Gates are also coached by Shpilband, who trained the top two junior dance teams as well. The United States has never won a world gold medal in ice dancing, but the Russian influence may very well lead them in that direction.

The current depth of the American team has made its national championship almost mandatory viewing to get an inkling of what will happen on world stages. It's not a new situation. American champions have won more Olympic skating medals than any other country – thirty-eight at last count. The United States has produced stars such as Dick Button, Peggy Fleming, Dorothy Hamill, Brian Boitano, Scott Hamilton, and countless others. During 1995-96, it became clear that the star-making machine of the United States was not even close to shutting down.

The European Championship

*E*uropean championships were a fixture in figure skating five years before the first world championship. The first European champi- onship, held in 1891, offered only a competition for seven men from two countries, Austria and Germany. Since then it has heralded the emergence of future skating stars. Nobody had heard of tiny Oksana Baiul of Ukraine before she won the 1993 European championship. And in 1995, a fresh-faced kid named Ilia Kulik of Russia staged a major upset to win the event; he is now one of the prime contenders for an Olympic medal in Nagano, Japan, in 1998. The 1996 European championship was held in Bulgaria from January 22 to 28.

There was no doubt about who ruled figure skating at the European cham- pionship in Sofia, Bulgaria. It was Russia, with three gold medals in its traditional domains of pairs and ice dancing and in its not-so-traditional sphere of women's skating.

The only gold Russia failed to garner was in the men's event, but there was good reason; its 1994 Olympic champion, Alexei Urmanov, was suffering

Irina Slutskaia of Russia loves to laugh. Her hobby is collecting stuffed animals, and, at last count, she has forty of them at her family's small Moscow flat. With her freshness, Slutskaia seems to have no ego problems. Of the battle between Michelle Kwan and Chen Lu at the world figure-skating championship, she said, "Both girls deserved to win."

(Page 99)
Maria Butryskaia

Alexei Urmanov showed up early in the season, ready to skate. This season, he had one advantage over others: after some money-making tours in the United States, he was able to buy himself a car. In previous years, it would take him one and a half hours to get to the rink. Because he had to do this twice a day, he spent six hours each day on buses. He was able to waste less time and energy during the 1995-96 season. He also avoided long tours, said his coach, Alexei Mishin. "He was able to organize physical-fitness training," Mishin added.

from conjunctivitis, an eye inflammation caused by a virus. In Sofia, Urmanov stood on the sidelines as Viacheslav Zagorodniuk (Slava to his friends) of Ukraine won his first European title after toiling quietly in the trenches behind the leaders for years.

Urmanov's condition was serious. The area around his eyes turned black and blue. "It was very, very strong," said Urmanov's coach, Alexei Mishin. "It was difficult to fight this disease." Mishin said the virus left the small muscles around Urmanov's eyes weak, so that he found it hard to focus. The problem began to bother him at the Nations Cup in Germany in November, when he finished second to Zagorodniuk. In all, Urmanov lost twenty-five days of training, also partly because of poor ice conditions. Any thought of Urmanov training quadruple jumps was dashed.

Still, in Sofia, the force was with Russia as three of its men finished within the top six: Igor Pashkevich, a forgotten world junior champion of 1990, who missed the 1995 season with a virus and infection that temporarily paralyzed half of his face, was second; boyish Ilya Kulik came close to losing his spot on the world team by finishing third, with a less-than-excellent free-skate; and Alexei Yagudin, only fifteen and Urmanov's training mate and stand-in, was sixth. All in all, Russian skaters won $156,000 (U.S.) – almost one-third – of the $470,000 prize money offered in this event.

Five years ago, Zagorodniuk would have been considered one of the Soviet flock, but he went through the vaunted system on a different path – away from the skating centers of Russia in Moscow and St. Petersburg, at a rink built only twenty-five years ago beside the balmy waters of Odessa, Ukraine. "It was a very strange position for schools to operate outside of Moscow," said his coach, Valentin Nikolaev, his eyes made owl-like by thick glasses. "For a long time, we tried to show our best job to Moscow."

But it was only when Ukrainian Victor Petrenko won the world junior championship in 1984 that the centers of Soviet skating took Odessa seriously, he said. In 1989, Zagorodniuk won the world junior title – a decade after his mother, a devotee of figure skating, urged him to take lessons to improve his hockey skills. Zagorodniuk, a lover of all sports, really wanted most to play hockey. Odessa, however, had no hockey club. Kiev, which did, was too far away for a young boy. In this way, hockey lost a player, but figure skating gained a European champion.

Currently, Zagorodniuk is best known for the traveling power of his triple Axel, which soars across the ice farther than all others, according to his coach.

"The first time I saw [Viacheslav Zagorodniuk], I was not sure if he'll be good skater," said his Ukrainian coach, Valentin Nikolaev. "But after three years, I saw this boy had beautiful position for jumping. It's more important for talent. He's not a big talent, but it's hard work. He's very clever. This is a very difficult sport for stupid people."

When Zagorodniuk launches his pencil-slim body into the air, he flies "about fifteen skate blades" – or about fifteen to sixteen feet (four or five meters) – over the ice before landing. He has been doing the difficult jump with three and a half rotations since he was fifteen years old. He is now twenty-three, with much less time for hockey pucks. In the summer of 1994, after he won a world bronze medal in Japan, Zagorodniuk married Ukrainian ice dancer Olga Mudrak. He says the marriage has given him confidence in skating.

If Zagorodniuk had finally hit his stride in Sofia, so did Russian pairs skaters Oksana Kazakova and Artur Dmitriev, and the delightful Irina Slutskaia, broad-faced, ruddy-cheeked, all giggles, and athletically daunting in the women's event.

"She's amazing. I love her," 1995 U.S. champion Nicole Bobek once said of Slutskaia. "At the Goodwill Games [in 1994], she had a terrible, terrible short program, and she came off the ice, came into the dressing room, threw her flowers, and was bawling her eyes out. I came over and gave her a big hug. She reminds me of a little sister. She's adorable."

Slutskaia inspires those feelings, although, during the past year, the world has seen few tears from the teenager, who lives at home in Moscow with her father, an auto-mechanics teacher, and her mother, who took her to the rink as a small child for health reasons. Her mother believed skating would help her become stronger and put an end to her constant colds. Growing up, Slutskaia admired not another female skater but 1988 Olympic champion Brian Boitano, whose powerful jumping style appealed to her.

She had known Midori Ito of Japan, another athletic skater, only as a legend, on television. That changed in Edmonton in March 1996, when she competed skate to skate with Ito for the first time. Slutskaia placed third to Ito's seventh.

In Sofia, Slutskaia never put a foot wrong. Dressed in sky-blue sparkle and feather puffs, with a girlish rope in her hair and no hint of make-up, she landed three combination jumps, including the difficult triple Lutz–double toe-loop, and an array of Biellmann spins, done with both feet and in several positions. The schoolgirl pulled four marks of 5.9 out of 6.0 from the steely-eyed judges. Three of them were for artistic impression, a measure of the joy with which she skates. With this undeniable effort, Slutskaia stopped veteran Surya Bonaly of France in her tracks. Bonaly had been seeking to win her sixth consecutive European title and, under pressure of criticism, had even ditched her long program and offered up a new one, *Swan Lake*, to the judges. She had to settle for silver.

Not even twenty-three-year-old Muscovite Maria Butyrskaia, with her exotic looks and serious, dramatic style, could match little Slutskaia that day. Butyrskaia won bronze and completed a rare Russian coup – Russian women taking two of three medals at the European championship. It had never happened before. And Slutskaia was leading the charge.

And if Slutskaia was a new, fresh face at the European championship, Artur Dmitriev was a familiar one. When Natalia Mishkuteniok, the partner with whom he had won the 1992 Olympic pairs-skating gold medal, chose to quit, learn English at a New York university, and get engaged to marry, Dmitriev decided he was not through with amateur competition. He had

Maria Butryskaia has always had to fight for her spot on Russian teams. In 1995, she lost out on the only world championship berth available to Russian women to Olga Markova. In 1995-96, there were two spots, but a three-way battle for them. This time, Butyskaia finally earned it, two months after she won the Russian championship. In Russia, there are no guarantees, even if you are a champion.

trials with five partnership candidates, excluding Marina Eltsova. Although a match-up with her was discussed, Dmitriev said he did not want "to crash" her successful alliance with Andrei Bushkov, with whom she had won the 1993 European championship.

Dmitriev knew little about the five women with whom he skated. But fortunately Oksana Kazakova became available, because the partner with which she had placed fourth at the Russian national championship was too small for her; there was not enough of a height and weight differential between them, making triple twists impossible. However, even after Dmitriev teamed up with Kazakova in February 1995, they were beset with a long series of frustrating setbacks.

The pair had worked together for only two weeks before Dmitriev took a fall while tossing Kazakova very high in a twist move. Kazakova, falling from more than ten feet (three meters) in the air, injured some ligaments in her right foot on impact. She was off the ice for three months. "She couldn't even jump," said coach Tamara Moskvina. Dmitriev also had to deal with a back problem – a compressed disk – which developed after the Lillehammer Olympics and was aggravated by constant practices with Kazakova in their rushed attempt to make up lost time. "I had no operation," Dmitriev said. "I had many meetings with the physiotherapist. I just did exercises."

"The stop and start was discouraging. [Kazakova] started doing difficult elements in July, but she had pain. So we just made programs. We had not too much time for practice."

With this series of problems, Kazakova and Dmitriev finished only fifth at Skate America in Detroit, Michigan, their first international competition together. It was an inauspicious debut. Between the two of them, they fell four times. One judge placed them last of seven.

"I feel miserable," Moskvina said candidly of their performance afterward. "They need more time. They want to skate on the level of Olympic participants, but it's rather difficult. Maybe I was too adventurous to put them in this event so soon. But those who don't risk, don't drink champagne."

But by the time Kazakova and Dmitriev arrived in Sofia, more than two months later, they acted like a different pair. They acted like European champions. Kazakova, who appeared workmanlike at Skate America, blossomed in Sofia. "She is much more expressive than [Mishkuteniok]," Moskvina said. "With [Mishkuteniok], we did a lot of programs where she was just quietly beautiful. With Oksana, we would like to make new programs, but it has been difficult and time-consuming just to learn all new elements."

Kazakova seemed to find the time. In Sofia, she lit up the rink with her radiant smile. Although the pair made constant use of the elements for which Mishkuteniok and Dmitriev were famous, it was clear that a powerful force was emerging. The new pair landed all of the difficult elements, including side-by-side triple toe-loops, and missed only a triple twist, which never got off the ice. "I just forgot how to do it," Dmitriev said.

Artur Dmitriev's new partner, Oksana Kazakova, was not as innately flexible as her predecessor, Natalia Mishkuteniok. She had to work hard and long to develop the stretch that enables her to do the moves in these photos. Inevitably, Kazakova had to endure comparisons to Mishkuteniok, never more so than when she and Dmitriev faltered at the world championship. But the arresting pair barely had time in an injury-prone season to find their own niche in the skating world. They have only just begun.

In spite of their miscue, Dmitriev won his third European championship, his first with Kazakova. And they dethroned European defending champions Mandy Woetzel and Ingo Steuer of Germany.

But the Russians aren't finished yet. Dmitriev's former partner, Natalia Mishkuteniok, has teamed up with her love interest, U.S.-born hockey player Craig Shepard, as a pair, intent on performing in shows and eventually competing. Shepard played hockey at Michigan State, in minor leagues, and, for a time, even for the famous Moscow Dynamo hockey club. Their choreographer? Nina Petrenko, wife of 1992 Olympic champion Victor Petrenko. It is the stuff of movies. Both have seen the American film *The Cutting Edge*, in which a figure skater is matched up, rather unwillingly, with a hockey player. Against all odds, they become Olympic champion pairs skaters.

The Soviet pairs drama continued in Sofia. Legendary sixty-something Olympic champions Ludmila and Oleg Protopopov performed an exhibition at the European championship – perhaps as a tune-up for their newest project. The first Russian pair to win an Olympic or world gold medal dreamed of reinstating as amateurs with the hope of representing Switzerland – which currently has a drastic dearth of pairs – in the 1998 Nagano Games.

The problem is that the Protopopovs, who are regarded as ineligible skaters, had not asked for reinstatement to eligible status before the final deadline on April 1, 1995. Although skating networks were abuzz with the Protopopovs' hopes, International Skating Union official Beat Häsler said the pair has never requested reinstatement – and even if they were to reinstate, they would probably not pass the strict criteria of the Swiss Olympic Committee to get to the Nagano Games.

The Protopopovs, who defected from the Soviet Union in 1979 and settled in Switzerland, won their first Olympic gold medal in 1964 and their first world gold in 1965, beginning the Russian dominance of pairs skating. By the time of the next Olympic Games, Ludmila will be sixty-one years old, Oleg, sixty-four. There may be many Russian pairs skaters, but there is only one pair like the Protopopovs.

*T*he first official Canadian championship was held in 1914. Before that, dating back to 1905, various clubs in Canada would simply announce they were holding national championships without checking with any kind of central body. Eighty-two years after the first official event, Canadian championships are serious business, indeed. They are the ultimate test for skaters in the largest figure-skating association in the world, with almost two hundred thousand members. Like the U.S. championship, the Canadian event determines the country's representatives at the following world championship or Olympic Games. On its own merits, it is the crowning jewel of an industry that thrives in Canada. While five to six years ago the skating industry in Canada generated $20 million in economic activity, the skating business in the country is currently estimated to be worth $130 million.

Take risks. That was the important message the Canadian Figure Skating Association (CFSA), delivered months before 268 qualified athletes headed for their February national championship in Ottawa, all with buffed-up

"It felt magic," said Jean-Michel Bombardier, after he and pairs partner Michelle Menzies landed triple Salchows for the first time in the short program. The pair, in winning their second consecutive Canadian title, also earned a 5.9. Finally, after four years, they have found their step. "Because we worked on our triple jumps, I think our pair skating did suffer a little bit [early in the season]. But in the long run, it will make us a better team. We decided to commit ourselves to that triple jump and maybe suffer for a year."

(Page 111)
Victor Kraatz and
Shae-Lynn Bourne
(Facing page)
Elvis Stojko

Stéphane Yvars finished sixth in Canada, but was one of the few to land triple-Axel combinations. That he competed at all was a miracle. Once tabbed as a most promising young skater, Yvars dropped out of sight after 1990 with a serious knee injury that required surgery, which didn't work. After a skating comeback failed, he quit skating for one and half years. But under coach Doug Leigh's guidance, Yvars is back with a purpose.

skates and streamlined costumes in hand. They called the CFSA epistle the "memo," or the "letter," and everybody knew that it was the notice that demanded results from headquarters. "Talent is not the issue," said CFSA director-general David Dore. "The progression of it is."

The "letter" urged risk-taking – no holding back on the difficult elements needed to get to the top. Other countries had fifteen-year-old Michelle Kwan, or thirteen-year-old Nadejda Kanaeva, or sixteen-year-old Guo Zhengxin, or fourteen-year-old Takeshi Honda, all shaking off their childhood charms to reach for the stars. "We are being externally driven," said Dore, eyeing the tough competition. It was clear that, with one gold medal at the Birmingham world championship in 1995 and an astonishing lack of triple Axels, Canada was in a lull, spoiled by its roaring successes in the past decade. It was time, Dore figured, to get tough.

Suddenly, it became more difficult in 1995-96 to get onto the national team; there would be no international assignments for those who did not finish within the top five at a Canadian championship. The previous season, a top-eight achievement was the cut-off point to get onto the national team. And even with the placements, the skaters had to perform to get the top assignments. Men had to do triple Axels or at least attempt them with tenacity. Women wouldn't make it with a triple Salchow or two; they needed all the tough triples. The skaters buckled down to work.

It seemed to pay off. While no triple Axels had been seen in the long programs at the previous Canadian championship in Halifax, Nova Scotia (where Stojko withdrew with an injury partway through the short program), the capacity crowd saw seven men in Ottawa attempt triple-Axel combinations in the short program. Only two – Stojko and training mate Stéphane Yvars – landed them without breaking a sweat. Matthew Hall, the elder statesman of the group at age twenty-eight, landed one, but not securely enough to squeeze in a loop combination he had planned.

In the long program, half of the field of eighteen tried the triple Axel, but only two succeeded: Stojko and Jean-François Hébert, although the Quebec skater tried to make it into a combination that fizzled. Stojko also had to steady himself when he tried a second triple Axel in combination and put a foot down in error. Indeed, the king was not perfect in Ottawa, stumbling out of a quadruple attempt. "I'm human just like anybody else," he said. "The Canadian championship is a small part of what I want to do."

Still, the men's event was dogged with controversy. There was no disputing Stojko's easy win (although his stylist, Uschi Keszler, was in tears after the short program, believing that Stojko should have drawn a perfect mark of 6.0 for his presentation of the auto-racing speedway program), but the placements of the top half-dozen males kept discussions among officials and coaches buzzing for weeks after the event. Some thought judges did not actually reward skaters for attempting the difficult elements, in spite of "the letter."

"I've been hearing all year that we were supposed to be doing triple Axels, and I did one, but my mark is 4.4," Matthew Hall said. (Hall was placed as high as fifth by one judge, as low as twelfth by another.) Stéphane Yvars fell on a triple Lutz in the short program, but one judge gave him credit for trying the triple Axel in combination by placing him third. Many of the rest placed him seventh. Sébastien Britten finished second without attempting a triple Axel in the short program, but his programs are exquisite, sophisticated, world-class

Jean-Francois Hébert, once a Canadian bronze medalist

After disaster in the short program at the world championship, Sebastien Britten found his brightest moment during the long program, when he skated perhaps the most uplifting routine of his career. He got a standing ovation. "I was very close to crying when I finished," Britten said. "I couldn't believe the noise and the emotion. I wish I could thank every single person." He finished seventeenth, but marks didn't matter.

works, with difficult entries into jumps, well-choreographed elements and steps, and a flair for sensitive movement in harmony with music. Britten can accomplish more with the simple sweep of an arm than most others can by beating the air like windmills.

At issue in discussions was Marcus Christensen, who skated the best programs of his career to choreography and music that suited him well, but he attempted no triple Axels at all and still finished third, earning the trip to Edmonton for the world championship. His ordinals ranged from second to eighth.

The skater that may have suffered the most from lack of rewards was Jeffrey Langdon, who landed two triple-triple combinations in his long program, including a triple Salchow–triple loop, a feat that hadn't been seen since Kurt Browning landed them during his reign as world champion. And

Halfway through the season, Elvis Stojko scrapped his free-skate routine to music from The Last of the Mohicans *(pictured here) in favor of the previous year's program. "The [Mohican] program just didn't quite gel," he said. "The whole intent of the music is to talk about a group that is almost extinct. Every time I put the music on, I couldn't figure out why it was pushing me down. I had to work against it. You want music that lifts you."*

although he didn't land one in competition, the twenty-year-old grittily attempted triple Axels at every event, every practice. The biggest prize Langdon won was a rubber hand that someone threw to him jokingly in lieu of flowers after his long program. He finished fourth and missed the trip to Edmonton.

Fifteen-year-old Daniel Bellemare also showed boyish moxie, but he finished fifth.

Aside from the placements, much of the talk at the national championship centered around Stojko deciding to ditch the *Last of the Mohicans* routine that he used to win the NHK Trophy and go back to his long program of the previous year: the *1492: Conquest of Paradise* soundtrack.

"The other program didn't gel," Stojko says of the *Mohicans* routine. "The concept of the music is tragic, and I could sense that I had to work against

Susan Humphreys (right) and Canadian champion Jennifer Robinson (left) represent the future of women's skating in Canada. "I was a bit shaky, but I pulled myself together," said Humphreys of her bronze-medal finish in Ottawa. "I fought through the whole program and put in an extra triple. It was not the performance of a lifetime, but this year I was probably not really ready to be there [on top] any way." Humphreys is best known for her spectacular spiral (right). Robinson rose from the pre-novice level to become Canadian champion in only six years.

the music to get through it. But when we went back to last year's music, from the first few weeks, it grew."

Some of the most delightful programs of all were those of Josée Chouinard, the three-time Canadian champion, who had taken advantage of the ISU's last call for professionals to reinstate. Wanting to take one more crack at a world medal that had always eluded her, Chouinard came back and had to fight for only one berth that was allotted to Canadian women for the world championship in Edmonton.

After a year of toiling, however, Chouinard's quest fell short when her triples unraveled into doubles and spills in Ottawa. She landed only one triple jump, a Lutz – one of the most difficult – toward the end of her long program. Three of nine judges still placed her first, the other six voted for Jennifer Robinson, the brightest light to shine in a dismal women's event marked by constant tumbles. "The women's event was not a barn-burner," admitted David Dore. "It's the first time we've had a gutsy lady in a long time."

A tearful Chouinard was whisked out a back exit before anyone could speak to her, but her coach, Louis Stong, remarked that he was in shock, and Chouinard herself looked as if she had just been in a car wreck. "Her warm-up was bad, and skating first was bad, but there are no excuses," he said. "She blew it, period."

Stong said Chouinard's sights might have been set past the national championship, instead of on the event itself.

Robinson, enchanting with a sprinkle of freckles across her nose and a buoyant sense of humor, was unsure whether to cry with tears of joy or sadness; Chouinard had become a close friend. She apologized to Chouinard on the podium. Both were in tears. Susan Humphreys, still trying to regain her form after a serious back injury, was more stoic. She snatched the bronze, and, with her pure line and speed, promised better things for next season.

The senior women's event was one of the worst seen in recent memory; almost all of the competitors toppled like bowling pins, falling prey to pressure and expectation, failing to pick up the torch from a line of high-class Canadian female competitors, such as Barbara Ann Scott, Petra Burka, Karen Magnussen, and Elizabeth Manley. Canadians watched in stunned silence, wondering what happened.

"Everybody has been hard on the ladies' skating [in Canada], and it hasn't given them a lot of confidence," said Robinson's coach, Doug Leigh, who

*Canadian ice-
dancing champ
Shae-Lynn Bou
and Victor Kra
are best known
their low-to-the
moves, which fl
in the face of the
dancing conven
of skating with
erect bearing. D
the 1995-96 sea
Bourne and Kra
were told they s
too much time
this novelty mo
Other skaters, l
U.S. champions
Elizabeth Puns
and Jerod Swal
bronze medalis
Chalom and M
Gates, as well
Nicole Bobek an
Eric Millot,
have incorpora
similar moves.*

Just before the season started, Chantal Lefebvre's ice-dancing partner, Patrice Lauzon, told her he did not want to skate with her anymore. Instead, he teamed up with Marie-France Dubreuil. After that, Lefebvre teamed up with Canadian silver medalist Michel Brunet (shown here), whose partnership with Jennifer Boyce had ended. Now Lefebvre is competing against her former partner. "It was difficult for Chantal the first time she skated against him in divisionals [leading to the Canadian championship]," Brunet said. " Now it's fine." Dubreuil and Lauzon finished sixth at the Canadian championship. Lefebvre and Brunet finished second and earned a trip to the world championship.

Kristy Sargeant and Kris Wirtz were determined not to miss a berth on the world championship team, even after a nasty fall in practice at the Canadian championship. Wirtz was taken to hospital suffering from a concussion after he caught an edge while attempting a two-handed lift. In trying to cushion his partner's fall, Wirtz's head snapped backward onto the ice. Sargeant wrenched a knee and also suffered cuts and scrapes to her shoulder and elbow. They skated the long program the next day, but had to stop partway through when a false fire alarm in the arena interrupted their routine. They made it to the world championship and finished a strong seventh.

helped Robinson advance quickly from pre-novice level to Canadian senior champion in only six years. "More of them are trying triple Lutzes than ever before. The world is getting better, but you need to give them confidence and give them a chance to grow into themselves and develop. There's not a coach in this country that isn't trying to make ladies' skating better. Patience is the key. You give them experience, and experience gives them confidence.

"There were a lot of tough days out there before the cowboy hat," said Leigh, referring to the white hat Manley donned after her silver-medal performance at the 1988 Olympics in Calgary. "It didn't come without some hard and rigorous days."

Leigh's Mariposa skating club in Barrie, Ontario, delivered three of the four senior champions: Stojko, Robinson, and pairs skaters Michelle Menzies and Jean-Michel Bombardier, who successfully defended their 1995 title by landing – for the first time – triple Salchows in the short program, and showing speed, good technique, and a charismatic quality that went beyond both.

With Stojko watching at rinkside, Shae-Lynn Bourne and Victor Kraatz won their fourth senior national ice-dancing title with a standing ovation and four marks of 5.9 out of a perfect 6.0 for presentation. Under their shadow sprang Chantal Lefebvre, only eighteen, and Michel Brunet, twenty-five, a former Canadian silver medalist when he skated with Jennifer Boyce. Lefebvre and Brunet, together only six months, earned the silver medal and offered an entertaining alternative as Canada's ice dancers jockeyed for position behind the perennial leaders.

At least they pleased the captains of the CFSA. And that was tough to do.

China: A Rising Power

During the 1995-96 season, defending world champion Chen Lu of China established herself as a skater of rare sensitivity and charm, winning her first perfect marks of 6.0 for the quiet beauty of her performances. Her countrymate, young Guo Zhengxin, was best at another aspect of skating, a youthful, precocious athleticism that set the world on its heels. Yet nobody had heard of him before this season, and skating was still seen as a minor sport in China. With the guarantee of new rink construction in the near future, China, with its population of 1.2 billion, promises to be a vast and daunting power in figure skating in years to come.

In 1985, Zhang Shubin surprised everybody.

Out of the mysterious northern backwaters of China he came, from a country that revered its light-footed table-tennis players and gave no hint of dreams of winter sport. But Zhang, somehow, knew how to skate, knew what a triple Axel was, and had a pair of western skates on his feet, at least when he appeared internationally. Tall, with trusting dark eyes, he jumped not with the utmost grace but with the utmost height and power, right into fifth place

When Chen Lu stayed at choreographer Sandra Bezic's house in Toronto for two weeks in the summer of 1995, Bezic's family all fell in love with her. "She was a total delight and very hungry to be with a family," Bezic said. "I think she really missed it. She left her family at such a young age." One day, Chen disappeared. But she returned with an armful of groceries and cooked dinner for Bezic, her husband, Dino Ricci, and son, Dean. "Nobody ever does this," Bezic said. "She was very special."

of nine entries at Skate Canada in London, Ontario, in late 1985. The first Chinese skater to compete at Skate Canada in its eleven-year history, Zhang actually finished fourth in the long program, behind Josef Sabovcik of Czechoslovakia and Grzegorz Filipowski of Poland. The western world had never seen his like before, especially not from China.

The growth of figure skating in China has been a late project of its diligent people. China quietly became a member of the International Skating Union as far back as 1956. But Chinese skaters did not compete at a world championship until 1980 in Dortmund, West Germany, when the pairs team of Bo Luan and Bin Yao finished fifteenth of fifteen (after being together for only three months); Wang Zhili was last of twenty-two behind Jan Hoffman of Germany, and Liu Zhiying was last of twenty-nine behind Anett Poetzsch of East Germany. However, by 1995, the country of 1.2 billion people had produced its first world champion, Chen Lu. The world wondered: Was Chen Lu an anomaly? Was she a marvelous freak of nature, with her delayed tripling rotations, her soft, floating arms, her lightness over the ice, her balletic way?

Probably not, judging by the way the Chinese work. "It is only a matter of time," said Evelyn Li, who acted as translator for the tiny Chinese delegation to Skate Canada in 1985.

"You can count on it that they will come in well prepared," said Canadian diving coach Donald Webb, who watched the Chinese domination in diving rise during the 1980s. "They'll scramble for the first four or five years, but then they will be a threat. Believe me. They pick sports that are gymnastics-oriented. Diving was the first where they made their world mark. It wasn't long before they came in on gymnastics, and now they're one of the top powers there. Figure skating would be a natural for them. They'll be strong in jumps."

His words could have been prophetic. In November 1995, an unknown Chinese skater named Guo Zhengxin landed the first quadruple toe-loop – with ultimate ease – at the world *junior* figure-skating championship in Brisbane, Australia. In addition, he peppered his long-program routine with an extraordinary list of difficult triples: two triple Lutzes, a triple flip, and a triple Salchow in combination with a triple toe-loop. Just for good measure, he landed a quad in combination with a triple toe-loop in practice. Young Guo won the bronze medal, but his spins were weak and his artistic marks low.

And there are at least four or five more boys like him at home in China, according to Li Mingzhu, coach of Chen Lu. "There is a boy who is twelve

Zhang Shubin,
leading the
Chinese way

Guo Zhengxin startled the world when he showed up at the world junior championship with a quadruple jump. He landed another one in combination during the qualifying rounds at the world championship in Edmonton. The skater from Harbin finished third in his round, but a Finnish judge sent a firm message: he gave Guo an artistic mark that was 0.9 below his technical.

or thirteen who is landing quads. You just can't believe it, he is so small," she said. Still, China has only four hundred to five hundred figure skaters to choose from — so far. By comparison, Canada has almost two hundred thousand.

Webb says the Chinese — no matter what the sport — work with uncommon diligence to learn every aspect. No stone is left unturned. He found out just how painstaking are their efforts when, by chance, he took an elevator ride with them at a diving meet in Florida during the early 1980s, a couple of years after they first showed up at the 1979 World University Games in Mexico. As Webb stood next to a huddle of Chinese coaches in the lift, they suddenly turned to each other and spoke with some excitement in Chinese. Through an interpreter, they told Webb that they recognized him.

"How?" asked Webb, who had been the coach of Canadian diver Beverly Boys, who finished fourth at the 1968 Olympics.

They told him that he was the one who "pushed a button."

It suddenly occurred to Webb that what they had seen was a film clip that Speedo had sponsored in 1976 about the Olympic Games, which took place in Montreal that year. In the clip, Webb had indeed pushed a button to start up a bubble machine. "I appeared on that for only two seconds, and I had been standing in the background," he said. "Nobody should have recognized me. I'm amazed that they could pick me out of that well enough to recognize me on an elevator. But when you watch a film five thousand times, you know everything."

In the beginning, Webb said, Chinese divers had a reputation for turning in stellar practices, but they flopped during competition. By 1984, they were winning gold medals in diving. The nation seemed to have gone from zero to sixty almost overnight.

Skating, however, had a slow start in China. It takes ten to fifteen years to develop a top-level, elite skater, longer than to produce a competitor in almost any other sport. It didn't help that, in China, figure skating first developed not in the major urban centers, with their hot, humid summer climes, but rather in the northern provinces, with frigid winters that allowed natural ice – at least for five to six months of the year. But skating was not completely new to China when Zhang took to the blades and divers were flipping into pools. According to Don Laws, a U.S. figure-skating coach who spent three weeks in China in 1980 teaching and giving seminars, Chinese sport bodies had brought in skating coaches from other countries as far back as the 1930s. A Czech coach worked in China during the 1960s, too, Laws said. In recent years, Russian coaches have visited, leaving behind a wealth of coaching and training techniques and knowledge.

Still, skating in China was a minor sport that went completely dormant between 1966 and 1970 because of the oppressive political climate of Mao's Cultural Revolution. During the early 1970s, a few enthusiasts tried to revive it, but only in the chilly northeastern part of the country. According to the Chinese delegation to Skate Canada in 1985, it was only after 1979 that the Chinese began building arenas, and even those did not favor skating.

"They are not as good as the facilities you have here," said Sun Jiaqi, who was the co-chairman of the skating judges' committee in China in 1985 and also the secretary of the Harbin Club of Heilongjiang province, where Zhang started to skate. "The arenas were multi-purpose facilities, so you cannot expect them to be of world standard. You can't guarantee that you will be able to skate when you want, and they don't keep the ice as good. Sometimes they need the facility for basketball or other sports. Everybody has to adjust and give in a little."

Just before the building started to take place, winter-sport officials from China began to observe figure skating outside the country. A four-person mission showed up in Ottawa in 1978 to watch the world championship. While they were there, they approached United States Figure Skating Association officials to pursue a coaching exchange, but it never came to pass, apparently mired in red tape. Laws, then president of the Professional Skaters Guild of America (PSGA), an association of coaches, heard about the Ottawa request, and an idea was born. In relatively quick time, fifteen months after he approached the Chinese embassy in Washington, D.C., Laws and PSGA vice-president Fritz Dietl were on their way to Beijing (formerly Peking). They spent three weeks in China in April 1980, teaching rules, basic skating, jumping, off-ice training techniques, and music interpretation to the Chinese. They even did a session on nutrition.

In a letter dated September 13, 1979, an unidentified official from the Winter Sports Association in China had told Laws that there were only about three hundred skaters in the country, with fifty of them training intensively. "But their technical skills leave much to be desired," the letter read. Laws and Dietl were informed that the skaters used British-made skates, all training was done on outdoor rinks, and that if the Americans wished to use video equipment to teach, they had none to offer; the winter-sport body had to share a Sony video machine with other sports associations on the street.

In the early days of its appearance on the world stage, Chinese skating was "really kind of hokey," said Frank Carroll, who has coached Chen in California from time to time. "Their dresses were too long, their style was old-fashioned, and their freeleg was bent." A pair that appeared at the 1981 world championship in Hartford, Connecticut, struggled through their long program, the male lifting his tiny partner with difficulty, skating slowly and awkwardly. They could not spin, especially not simultaneously. And they could not help but see their competition, Russians and East Germans, sure and strong, tossing off throw double Axels with abandon. On a day of obvious anguish, the Chinese boy unknowingly skated the five-minute long program with his fly undone.

"When they first came out and were entering competitions, they were really quite raw," said Laws, who coached 1984 Olympic champion Scott

Pairs coach Bin Yao, himself a world competitor

Hamilton. "They could do the elements, but not triples, and the double Axel wasn't there. And they were not quite sharp on the rules and regulations of the ISU. They translated the rules, but they didn't know how to interpret them. Things had progressed so quickly at that time in figure skating that we had meetings outside [of the ISU congresses] to clarify things. They weren't in on all of that."

The only way to proceed during his Beijing seminars, Laws thought, was to start on page one of the ISU rulebook and explain everything, right from the figures and basic skating. Trouble was, in April 1980, the Chinese had few skating terms in their vernacular. "What is a flying camel spin in Chinese?" Laws said. During his stay, the Chinese created their own words for the terms.

"We wore out three interpreters, because they couldn't understand what we were saying," Laws said. "They were young people who spoke beautiful English. But what's a choctaw in Chinese? It's a [western] Indian term. They all contributed equally to the process, but they just got tired. The seminars went from 8 a.m. to 6 p.m. for three weeks."

In Beijing, Dietl and Laws worked with thirty-two coaches, twenty judges, and sixty-eight skaters from all over the country. Every word was taped, and their rapt listeners took volumes of notes. The Americans found that the Chinese had no off-ice training programs at all, and decided it was important to teach, because they had ice only five months a year, few rinks, and poor equipment. They found the Chinese fascinated with ice dancing, because of what they saw at the 1980 Lake Placid Olympics, but when they tried to match the skaters up, they stumbled all over each other because they had no concept of skating as a mirror image. The Chinese had only begun pairs skating the previous year. In the fifteen years since, the Chinese have fielded only one dance couple at a world championship – in 1985, when Liu Luyang and Zhao Xiaolei finished eighteenth of nineteen skaters in Tokyo.

Generally, Dietl and Laws found the Chinese skaters in 1980 had skills at the level of novice and junior skaters in North America. Standards for skate sharpening and blade setting were pitifully low. There were almost no skate-sharpening machines, and they had nothing with which to clean skates. Dietl and Laws did, however, find the arenas first-rate and very large. Rinks in Beijing and Shanghai had seating for seventeen thousand to eighteen thousand people and were extraordinarily spotless. They also made first-class ice, with the best Zamboni machines available – and they knew how to use them, Laws said.

By 1985, Canadian figure-skating coach co-ordinator Carol Rossignol had her eyes opened during a two-month sojourn to Beijing on an exchange program supported by Sport Canada; she watched in disbelief as a family in the capital used a bicycle to move a couch, in much the same way that the country was struggling to develop world-caliber figure skating: with determination. Rossignol, whose father was Chinese, reported that, even though China had built more than five thousand sport facilities in the previous six years, there were still only seven skating clubs in the country and four hundred skaters. Still, national team skaters got all their training free, and coaches in Beijing's Capitol Gymnasium were paid a salary by the school.

In the Beijing school, skaters lived in a crowded residence, with five or six people to a room, Rossignol said. The rooms were so small that there was space only for beds and a couple of dressers.

Zhang Shubin was lucky to have grown up in Harbin, which had one of only four indoor rinks in China by 1985. The indoor rink at Beijing's Capitol Gymnasium was only a month old when Rossignol was in China. "They had to make maximum use of it," she said. "So they skated twenty-four hours a day. Of that, four hours were reserved for speedskating and twenty hours for figure skating. Many young children, nine or ten years old, skated at 2, 3, or 4 a.m. The day hours were reserved for the better skaters."

By 1985, when Zhang appeared, official Sun Jiaqi said there were fifty to sixty judges in China, but only one that had been approved by the International Skating Union to judge top-level international events. The first Chinese judge at a world championship was Yang Jiasheng, who judged the men's and pairs' events at the world junior skating championship in Kitchener, Ontario, in 1987. Yang was one of the panel of nine judges to award first-place marks to Rudy Galindo, over Todd Eldredge, in the long program at that event. And Yang first appeared at a senior world championship in Munich in 1991 to give his opinions in the women's event, won by Kristi Yamaguchi.

Yang also came from Harbin, where there was a figure-skating school, and found it easy to become the Chinese men's champion from 1956 to 1963; he was the only competitor, he said. At his best, he won his titles with only two double jumps and a handful of singles in his repertoires. How did he learn these jumps? Nobody taught him. "You just look at others and you know how to do it," he said. "It was not a big deal."

Yang is a doctor, and now head of the research department in a sports-medicine institute in Beijing.

After agreements were signed for Canadians to build rinks in China, about twenty members of the Chinese embassy in Ottawa wanted to learn how to skate. They wanted only the best teacher. So, in 1995, Canada's 1962 world champion, Donald Jackson (third from the left), took on the job. Second from the left is Zhang Yijun, China's ambassador to Canada. At the far right is his wife.

Zhang Shubin was part of the first wave of those who expressed renewed interest in the icy sport after the terrors of the Cultural Revolution. Sun Jiaqi had watched over Zhang since he began skating as an eight-year-old in 1974 in Harbin. As a youngster himself, years before, Sun had skated on natural ice outdoors and was an interested spectator when coach Wang Junxiang attracted sixty tots to his school in Harbin. It was not long before Zhang impressed him as being one of the best.

In 1978, only four years after he picked up the sport, Zhang began landing some triple jumps; at the time, there were only two or three other skaters in a country of one billion who could equal his efforts, Sun said. By 1985, there were about fifteen to sixteen, but by then Zhang was going after triple Axels, too, always one step ahead of the rest. "He can do a triple Axel," Sun said of Zhang in 1985. "Not well, but he can land it."

Zhang first appeared internationally at the world junior championship in Oberstdorf, West Germany, in 1982 and, considering that most Chinese skaters finished last at almost every event in those days, was a guiding light and an inspiration back home with his fourteenth-place finish among twenty-two entries. In fact, he actually finished eleventh in the long program, only four spots behind Victor Petrenko, who went on ten years later to become an Olympic champion.

In 1984, Zhang was eighth at the NHK Trophy in Japan, but the following year he won the skating event at the World University Games in Italy and finished fifth at the St-Gervais competition in France. Although he skated at the

1988 Olympic Games in Calgary (finishing twentieth), China never sent him to a senior world championship. In fact, after its dismal pre-Zhang performances during the early 1980s, China stated publicly that it would withdraw from competing at world senior championships until its skaters were more able to compete at a higher level. Mainland Chinese skaters were seen at only one world championship – in nearby Tokyo in 1985 – between 1983 and 1991, when tiny Chen Lu first made an appearance. Curiously, at the Tokyo event in 1985, China did not send Zhang; instead, Xu Zhaoxiao went and finished twenty-third of twenty-seven skaters. But with financial help from Olympic committees, Chinese skaters did attend Olympic Games, starting in 1980 in Lake Placid, with only two singles skaters. These skaters were aided by something that made all the difference to the Chinese: the host country paid the full expenses of the athletes.

Zhang's no-show status at world senior championships during the 1980s was not particularly surprising. "They don't send them to worlds because they have no money," said Sharon Lariviere, a Canadian coach who spent two months in the summer of 1987 on a provincial exchange between Alberta and Heilongjiang province, where Zhang trained. "They are so broke, you have no idea. Their skates are so atrocious. They just pick a pair of skates out of a box. When Zhang went on his first international, he got [quality] skates. [But at home] their skates were pretty awful. They didn't even get to clean their skates for competition, unless they went international, because shoe polish cost too much. The girls' skates were just about black."

Lariviere also said the skaters in her group each had one outfit, such as "an old grey track suit," and wore it every day for two months. The outfits were washed once a week, every Sunday, when the skaters were taken to the river in Harbin for recreation.

Another Canadian coach, Shelley Glazer-Clements of Saskatoon, also got a rare insight into skating in China the following summer, in 1988, as part of a two-month cultural exchange set up between the Canadian provincial government of Saskatchewan and Jilin, its sister province in China. Working in an area that was once known as Mongolia, south of where Lariviere coached, Glazer-Clements, too, saw dismal skating conditions. "They don't have the best equipment," she said. "A lot of the boys were in girls' skates and the girls in boys' skates. A lot of the blades were too small and not properly mounted."

Glazer-Clements found that all of her students who lived in a special skating school were well rested and well fed. "That's why their parents wanted them in sports schools," she said – so much so that some parents were willing to spend a month's salary just to get them involved in skating and accepted into sports schools by the time they were seven years old. But Lariviere often faced a wall of yawns during morning sessions with her thirty skaters. "They always seemed to be tired, not as healthy as they should have been," she said.

One day, a speedskating coach from the Netherlands, who was also visiting and teaching that summer at the Harbin school, sneaked into the dining room where the skaters ate and found them munching only on rice, she said. Fruits and vegetables did not seem to be on the menu. With some concern, the visitors actually brought up the problem with school authorities. To dispel the foreigners' fears, the sports school invited them to dine with the students one evening. "That was as phoney as a two-dollar bill," Lariviere said. "But the kids loved it because of the kind of food they were getting."

Just before she left, Lariviere also discovered why her students seemed tired: they skated with their own club after they trained with her, but their club's ice time at the summer school was scheduled for the wee hours of the morning.

Arenas also weren't perfect, in spite of what Don Laws and Fritz Dietl found, albeit in more modern urban centers like Beijing and Shanghai. "The arena we taught in was brand new, supposedly, a year old, but practically falling down," Lariviere said. "And we wouldn't have water for a week, so we wouldn't flood the ice. Then the pipes [beneath the ice] would start showing. It was horrible ice. The next week, we'd get water, but we wouldn't get electricity, so we'd end up with one lightbulb hanging in the middle of the arena."

The Harbin arena was massive, she said, with seating for as many as thirty thousand people. But the workmanship in it – and in other relatively new buildings in the province – was shoddy. "They haven't got the tools," Lariviere said. "They hang nets outside the buildings to catch the workers when they do work on the high-rises."

Skaters suffered injuries, too, both Canadian coaches said, but Chinese authorities appeared to pay little attention to these woes. One thirteen-year-old girl, weighing all of sixty pounds (twenty-seven kilograms), cut her chin one day while attempting a spin in Harbin. "I picked her up and she was really bleeding," Lariviere said. "She needed stitches." When Lariviere asked an interpreter to take the girl to a hospital, he demurred, saying, "We can't do that or she'll lose her spot on the national team. If she doesn't stay here, she'll get reprimanded." When Lariviere and another Canadian coach, Les Hill from Edmonton, threatened to leave the building until she was treated, the interpreter rushed off with the girl. He returned in only five minutes, with a stitched-up skater. "I had a feeling the rink men did it," Lariviere said. "I hung onto her the rest of the morning. Her eyes swelled up and she looked awful. They wouldn't let her go back to the dorm, because she'd lose her spot. The athletes had to put out or there would be someone else waiting behind the wall, saying, 'You're next.'

"They skated with bad knees and sprained ankles and they didn't say anything, these kids," Lariviere said.

Glazer-Clements said she did not want to speculate on what caused the injuries, but she tried to teach the Chinese coaches ways of reinforcing a positive self-image rather than using the critical method of teaching they tended to use. "We did a lot of dealing with the athlete as a person, rather than a machine," she said. "You can't beat somebody into achieving a goal. You can't make somebody land a triple Lutz. You don't keep hammering at it and possibly causing injury. There was a lot of criticism there. But some people have that philosophy even in our own country."

In spite of all the disadvantages skaters faced in China, both Glazer-Clements and Lariviere were astonished at the level of skating among their students. "I had never even heard of Harbin before I went," Lariviere said. "But there were seven million people and eleven universities there. We thought we'd be dealing with a bunch of people stumbling around, but we saw triple jumps all over the place.

"I had three nine-year-old boys that did triple Lutzes. They had skates that our kids would have put in the garbage pail. Kids just skated. Put them in the right direction and they'd skate to death. I have always thought our Canadian kids are too fussy.

"The first day, my mouth was hanging open. They have lots of really good athletes. We went into a session where there were sixty kids on the ice and half of them could do triple jumps. Little eight-year-olds could do double Axels. They were just snapping them out."

Rotating, turning, leaping aside, the Chinese skaters were lacking in some areas; they couldn't spin. Rossignol saw it. Lariviere saw it. "Spinning they didn't understand," Lariviere said. "It just wasn't important to them." Glazer-Clements agreed. The world saw it when Guo Zhengxin amazed all in Brisbane, Australia, with his jumps – but couldn't spin well. "And they had terrible programs," Lariviere said. "They didn't have any idea of music or

The Chinese pair of Shen Xue (right) and Zhao Hongbo finished fifteenth of twenty-three couples at the world championship, but even though they are China's only senior pair, they executed extremely difficult elements with brilliance and great height. A German judge ranked them eighth. They trained in the former Soviet Union for two and a half years in an exhange program.

choreography. They just lacked the finer details, the spit and polish and the music. Some of them just had dreadful music."

Interpretation of the music was another problem. Rossignol found, a few years earlier, that Chinese ice dancers were somewhat inhibited by their culture. Once, while she was trying to explain to a nineteen- and twenty-year-old couple that they must show feelings toward each other during a dance, Rossignol's Mandarin interpreter told her they were too young for such things.

"The kids were emotionless [on the ice]," Lariviere said. "We gave a choreography class, and we found that the hardest because we couldn't get through to them that they had to just let their hair down and just be what the music said. We tried so hard for about a week, and finally they seemed to catch on. They were so disciplined. And boring. You couldn't get them to smile. You couldn't get them to cry. But we brought a lot of music with us. They loved to jive and they loved to do the Charleston. They'd heard about it."

Off the ice, the Chinese were "the happiest people," Lariviere said. "They had nothing. They would live thirty to a room, but the park was their living room. In some parks there were twenty-five thousand people, all doing t'ai chi in the morning." And they were not shy with their affections, Glazer-Clements said. "They were wonderful. We loved each other. We were like one big happy family."

In fact, in the beginning Lariviere was amazed to see young skaters traveling from one end of the ice to the other *en masse*, never separately. "They'd all stand around and have their arms around each other," she described. "We had the worst time getting them to spread out. Every day, I'd ask them to spread out because I thought they were going to stab somebody when they'd check their leg back on a jump. They'd all be doing triple flips or something and they'd all go in a flock, down the ice, then they'd come up the ice, and they'd all be in this little flock. When you'd talk to them, they'd all squat down on their haunches, side by side, butt to butt, and they'd put their arms around each other. They're just very fine, very delicate."

And the women are "so fine," Lariviere said, that she is surprised to see the emergence of a Chen Lu at all. "On my provincial team, the girls just weren't tough enough," she said. "They were the weak spokes. When I went out to banquets in China, I was often the only woman at the table. The premier of the province didn't like me, because I was a woman. After we traveled together for about four days, he liked me." Lariviere said the premier at first refused to acknowledge her when they were sitting at the same table. It was because he was from the old school, and "you don't eat with women," she said. "This was really quite hard on him."

Chen Lu, smiling with her silver medal

In the end, the premier shook Lariviere's hand and mustered up the moxie to tell her he liked her dress. "It was very difficult at times, because they don't think women are anything," she said. "I think they treat their daughters and their wives like nothing. These children were quite humble. I had four or five young girls [in the summer school] that were very delicate, very, very pretty, but they weren't tough enough physically and mentally. They got frustrated too easily and gave up, and their coaches were pushing them. They had low self-esteem."

Figure skating seems to be a male-dominated sport in China. Both Lariviere and Glazer-Clements taught only about five girls in classes of thirty skaters during their tenure in China. "The sport in Canada is very female-oriented and it's hard to find a male," Glazer-Clements said. "But in China, they really promote the male skaters."

"And the boys had wonderful bodies," Lariviere said. "Their centers of gravity were just right for jumping."

Among the five girls that Glazer-Clements taught in the harsh northwestern city of Changchun was eleven-year-old Chen Lu, delicate, pretty, but not at all fazed by the pain of falling, trying, and training, in spite of poor skates, skating on an outdoor rink (Changchun had only one artificial ice surface at the time), with sessions that were held from midnight to 5 a.m., and in temperatures that often dipped to -22°F (-30°C).

"It was pretty evident, even at that time, that she was quite talented," Glazer-Clements said of the skater who had joined the club only four years earlier. "She was doing all her triples, except a triple Axel. At that age, she was already doing triple Lutzes. She had the tricks of a senior North American skater, but she had the strength of an eleven-year-old. She's very hard-working, and she loved her skating. It was more than just hard work. She had desire. With all of those positive aspects of her behavior, it just led to her being a very successful young lady."

Although Chen had had a good dose of ballet instruction when she was young in China, Glazer-Clements said that, even in her pre-teens, she "had a natural way of working with her body. She was by far outstanding when it came to her body language on the ice. Everybody got the same training. But her body positions, and the softness of her body and her line, she just excelled. The other four girls were really lovely to watch, but [Chen] had something special, like a little charisma. She had something hanging over her that made her special in her body movement."

Midori Ito of Japan was an early model for Chen Lu.

Chen was born into a sports family: her mother was a table-tennis coach; her father, Xiqin, a full-time hockey coach who had spent three years as a player with China's national team. Chen began skating in a flooded soccer field in her backyard at the age of four and a half, because she was not physically strong enough to try other sports. Her first pair of skates were second-hand boy's skates, because her parents could not find girl's skates to fit her. As it was, Chen had to pull two pairs of socks on her feet to make the boy's skates fit, she said.

A family friend who skated and her father were her coaches from the beginning. Under their watchful eyes, little Chen would start at 9 a.m. and wouldn't call it a day until 6 p.m. "I could have gone longer, but there wasn't any light," Chen – almost apologetically – told Toller Cranston, who designed her world-title-winning programs and costumes in 1995. "Nobody in North America at that age would have skated for that length of time," Cranston said in amazement.

Chen also told Cranston that she landed her first double Axel at age seven. How? Incredibly, she learned by watching films of the difficult jump, Cranston said.

Li Mingzhu, who finished fourth at the 1979 Chinese national championships, at about the same time that the world figure-skating championship began to be shown on television in her country, took over Chen's training at age six. But the girl's obsession cost her parents a lot of money for training and skates. She has two older sisters, who skate only for recreation. They all pooled their resources for Lu-Lu, as she is affectionately called in the western world.

Although few other skaters saw the inside of a non-Chinese rink, China was already pushing an eleven-year-old Chen to international events during the late 1980s. While Glazer-Clements was in China, Chen was being prepped for Moscow Skate, to compete against senior-level skaters.

At her first world (senior) championship in 1991, when she was only fourteen, the minimum age, Chen sported a twelfth-place finish, skating to music by the Beijing Orchestra. It was a big step, and an important one to a young skater just finding her feet among the Kristi Yamaguchis of the world; little Chen, wearing costumes stitched up by her long-time coach Li Mingzhu, cried with joy after her long-program performance, because she had accomplished what she wanted: facing an international stage. Modestly, she doesn't think of herself as a torch-bearer for Chinese skating. But she is.

A young Chen Lu admired Kristi Yamaguchi.

Li, who had started to skate in 1960 when the level of skating in her country was woeful, had few examples to teach artistry; but at least she knew of 1968 Olympic champion Peggy Fleming, the princess of beautiful skating, who had performed in Beijing during the early 1980s. And, most of all, Chen wanted to emulate Fleming. As a young girl, she had seen Fleming on a television special and had asked her father, "Who is this lady? She is so beautiful. I want be just like her. I want be world champion." Even though Li was an accomplished, knowledgeable coach, she knew she needed more outside help.

After a month's stay in Milan, Italy, in 1991 (financed by the Chinese government), where she sought the advice of master coach Carlo Fassi, Chen was skating in literally another world, to western music – love fantasies, Spanish fantasies – played by American philharmonic orchestras. Only a year later, at age fifteen, she won her first world medals – bronzes – at both the junior and senior world championships. At the world championship in Oakland, California, she stood on a podium next to Kristi Yamaguchi, who had been a childhood skating heroine. Midori Ito had also been an early role model.

After these successes, Chen said she left her parents and sisters behind in Changchun to train in the central sports school in Beijing. "It was hard," she said. She still sees her family seldom, although her mother traveled to Beijing to stay with her for a week during the summer following her world-title win.

"The thing about working with her is that she's a darling girl," Cranston said of his sessions with Chen during the 1994-95 season, when she blossomed, grew into a woman, and made *The Last Emperor* routine her own. "I had not actually encountered her kind of diligence or discipline. I had not bumped into that until I bumped into her. Very intense girl. Top of the line for discipline. The girl is like a teacher's dream. She is truly a miracle."

However, even after Chen won her first world title in Birmingham, England, in March 1995, with her parents watching the women's final live on satellite television in Changchun, there was little fanfare back home. She may be China's premier winter-sport figure, but Chinese people have not traditionally been very interested in winter sport. There were no front-page stories of her victory in China's government-controlled newspapers, although the *South China Morning Post* in Hong Kong ran the story on its front page, adorned with a large color photograph of Chen. The *Workers' Daily* merely mentioned Chen's feat in a small story on page eight, buried in columns of statistics.

However, throughout Asia, Chen's success has struck a chord; she has become such a popular figure that she now finds herself swamped by autograph-seekers at every turn, barely able to move or breath at Asian Games, the sporting event revered sometimes more highly than the Olympic Games in Asia. At home in China, she says her people are "very shy"; they would like to ask for her autograph, but they do not wish to intrude. Although she says her successes have encouraged more young children to take to the ice, skating, however, is still a minor sport in China.

That could change very quickly, particularly with an international agreement that was signed five months before Chen's win, during Canadian Prime Minister Jean Chrétien's first state visit to China in November 1994. Toronto-based businessmen Paul Goulet and partner Jack Grover of Pacific Entertainment Group Inc. signed a joint-venture twenty-five-year contract with China to build and operate indoor ice-sport complexes in four of the largest urban centers in the heavily populated country.

The first will be built in Shanghai, a humid delta city with Texas-like temperatures: 95°F (35°C) to 104°F (40°C) for six months of the year. Others will follow in the inland city of Chongqing; in Beijing (ten million people); and in Shenzhen, with a population of 2.5 million, that enjoys summerlike temperatures year-round and lies just across the bay from bustling, wealthy Hong Kong. All are in southern regions, with few – or no – skating facilities. As part of the deal, the Canadian Hockey Association and the Canadian Figure Skating Association offered the use of their skating programs in the new facilities.

"The Chinese government has targeted ice sport – speedskating, ice skating, and hockey – as what it wants to teach their schoolchildren," said David Dore, director-general of the CFSA. "They want to have all their schoolchildren learn ice sport and they wanted Canadian programs. . . . This deal kind of fell into our hands. My mouth just sort of dropped open."

How interested are the Chinese in skating? "Very," said Grover. "The government asked us what was the quickest way to develop the sport. We said the quickest way would be to make it part of [schoolchildren's] regular day. We found that China had been looking at ice sport, but were at a loss as to how to make the facilities pay for themselves. It doesn't cost them a lot to train an athlete if they have the facilities, but they don't have the facilities. . . . They basically want to have not one Chen Lu but thousands of them."

In the Beijing rink complex where Chen currently trains, Grover said he saw the ice falling six inches (fifteen centimeters) short of the dasher boards, which were rotting, leaving the concrete base to peek through ominously. "They don't think anything of it," he said. "They just don't skate to the edge. We would close it down, but they train on it." He said an older building on the site was not temperature-controlled, making it expensive to keep ice in it for long periods. Many of the rinks China currently has are used only for training, leaving recreational skating to take place on outdoor ice surfaces.

But is Canada throwing away its skating expertise to a country that may very well be able to dominate it in international competitive circles in the future? Dore said there will be benefits to the deal: although the programs are not being sold, the CFSA will earn revenues from sales of accoutrements attached to the programs, such as the badges skaters earn for passing certain tests. These revenues will help defray the costs of Canadian programs and skating development. With 20 per cent of the population attaining the *nouveau riche* category in China, according to Grover, with the trend toward pampering the young, and with children forming one-third of China's population, the financial prospects seem enormous.

Many of Goulet and Grover's rinks – each with two pads, one Olympic-sized and set to operate twenty-four hours a day – will be located in high-traffic downtown areas. The Shanghai rink will be located in a school district, with 3 million children situated within a fifteen-minute walk of the rink, Grover said. He estimates that 160 children every hour will be bussed into the rink to take skating lessons. From 9 a.m. to 4 p.m., during each school day, the rink is expected to attract one thousand to two thousand children – or five thousand children a week. Factory workers will use the ice in off hours. Within five years, Grover estimated there could be 5 million people skating in China.

The Shanghai rink is expected to open during the winter of 1997. It will cost $9 million, with the money coming from private sources.

Pacific Entertainment will hire Canadian builders, construct the rink to Canadian specifications, hire the coaching staff – Canadian coaches will spend six months to a year in Shanghai to get the programs off the ground – and operate pro shops, which will eventually sell skates and other related products in a region where such things are as scarce as snowbanks. (The first year, customers will be given the use of skates as part of their learning fee, Grover said.)

About half a year before the first rink opens, sixty young Chinese skaters, sons and daughters of Shanghai politicians and the cultural elite, will spend two months in Canada, learning how to play hockey and to skate with toe picks, all with the idea of training them for a special opening-night exhibition, so the Chinese may watch their own on blades. It is intended to form a rousing start to a long Chinese love affair with the ice.

It will only be a beginning. When Zhang appeared at Skate Canada in 1985 with some mysterious Chinese letters on his track suit, it was a start, too. One letter was the figure for China, the other for the word "middle."

"China is a middle country," explained his Chinese translator, Evelyn Li. "The people are neither aggressive nor passive."

But they are many, and diligent, and made for figure skating.

The Champions Series Final

*T*his new International Skating Union event for eligible or amateur skaters, held in Paris, France, from February 23 to 25, 1996, set the stage for the world championship three weeks later in Canada. Although there had been concerns that the Champions Series final would eventually eclipse the world championship, or at the very least upstage it, most skaters at the Paris event made it clear that the world championship remained their primary focus.

The Champions Series final was a place for the Russians to flex their muscles atop shiny blades, and so they did: Russian skaters won three of four gold medals, six of twelve medals offered, and $345,000 (U.S.) of the $660,000 prize money.

Tiny Michelle Kwan, suited up as Salome, little baubles glinting from each side of her exotic eyes, was alone in breaking the Russian stronghold, although during practices she looked anything but a threat; no skater fell so often or so hard that week. But she also practiced more often than most in the days leading up to the competition.

On August 7, 1995, Evgenia Shishkova married her Russian pairs partner, Vadim Naumov. In the beginning, Naumov wasn't at all sure this would ever happen. "I always thought she was very funny," Naumov said. "And she was very pretty. She is even more pretty now. But she didn't like me in the beginning. For me, it was a little bit nervous. I had to prove to her that [I am good for her]." The wedding was small, with only family and friends. They had no honeymoon, only three or four days of relaxing.

(Page 145 and facing page)
Oksana Grischuk and Evgeny Platov

"We're just trying to get her body going quicker again to recover from being sick," said her coach, Frank Carroll, speaking of the illness that had plagued her during the Centennial on Ice competition the previous week in St. Petersburg. Kwan had had an unusual dip in her career in the Russian event, where she finished only third.

"She was very, very weak in Russia and coughing her lungs out," Carroll said. "I'm glad she was sick there. If we had to choose one to be sick at, it was there, because by [the world championship in] Edmonton, she should be fine. Every day [in Paris], she's gotten better. Her freestyle practices [by the end of the week] were very good. I could see her timing coming back."

It was just in time. Kwan fell on a triple toe-loop during the short program, which was won by Chen Lu, and was in only fourth position going into the long program. Chen faltered badly in the long; Kwan rose to the occasion, while Chen dropped to fourth, out of the medals. What happened? "Bad day," Chen said, trying to look bright.

Russia was such a power in the final that it was the only country to field three competitors in the women's event: Maria Butyrskaia, Irina Slutskaia, and Olga Markova. Slutskaia just qualified, finishing in a tie with Markova for the sixth position. When officials could not break the tie, they accepted a seventh woman into the event, which was originally intended for only six. Slutskaia took advantage of it and won silver with her solid jumping ability and enchanting spins.

Josée Chouinard of Canada won bronze, but for the twenty-six-year-old skater, it was a victory of sorts, the podium position she sought in her comeback as an eligible skater. After a tearful week at home, having missed qualifying for the world championship, Chouinard came to Paris fighting, but jittery.

"I've never seen her that nervous, almost to the point of throwing up," said her coach, Louis Stong. "She wanted to prove to herself that she could still do it under pressure. She showed big guts at the end [of the long program], substituting a triple toe-loop for a double Axel. Considering what she's been through, a bronze medal at this level is pretty good."

Chouinard was left feeling proud of herself, saying she could return home with her head held high. "I know I could have done a little better," she said, speaking of her misses on two triple Lutzes, a bobble on a triple flip, and a doubling of a toe loop. "But this week, I was very aggressive, very determined. Not long ago, I was down on myself. But I did the podium in a way."

Olga Markova of Russia lost out on a battle to gain a world-championship berth. The twenty-two-year-old skater, who had been ranked second in Russia in 1995, dropped to third in 1996. A silver medalist at Skate Canada in 1993 and at the European championship in 1995, Markova's fortunes tumbled during the 1995-96 season. She finished only eleventh at the European championship in Sofia after making two major errors in the short program. She is trained by Elena Vodorezova, the first Soviet woman to win a world championship medal (bronze in 1983).

By Paris, Chouinard appeared to be leaning toward continuing her career on the professional level, setting aside for good her dream of winning a world medal.

Other Canadians left Paris disappointed. After two consecutive years of coaching changes, and after a season of controversy over the content of their programs, Shae-Lynn Bourne and Victor Kraatz finished fourth and last, after having finished third in the *paso doble*, ironically a dance for which they had earlier drawn criticism. And two-time world champion Elvis Stojko was left with the silver medal in the men's event, behind Russian Alexei Urmanov. No Canadians qualified for the pairs event.

Russians dominated the dance and pairs events, as is their custom, with Oksana Grischuk and Evgeny Platov winning the dance, and Evgenia Shishkova and Vadim Naumov the pairs. And Urmanov, of course, was in an unbeatable mode in the men's event, winning both the short and the long programs on the strength of his presentation and athletic ability.

Urmanov emerged the winner in the short program in Paris as one of only two skaters to land a triple Axel–triple toe-loop combination. (Viacheslav Zagorodniuk was the other.) Stojko landed only a triple-double. At one point, with the way the ordinals were changing, Stojko thought he might be as far down as fourth of six entries after the short program, but with others making mistakes, he ended up second after this phase.

The long-program placements were even more interesting. Stojko stumbled out of three jumps, but, when he landed a quadruple toe-loop, all but one judge awarded him top technical marks. (The other one, a Japanese judge, tied Stojko and Urmanov, who had made fewer mistakes.) Judges also noticed that Stojko skated out of his jump landings with more flow than Urmanov at this event.

The race came down to presentation, and clearly presentation won out. All but one judge, including a Canadian judge, awarded top presentation marks to Urmanov in the long program. Overall, four of seven judges did not think that Stojko's quadruple overcame his misses – and his presentation.

The men's event was seen as a rematch of the 1994 Olympic Games, in which Urmanov defeated Stojko with higher artistic marks. The prevailing assumption about both results was that the judges preferred Urmanov's classical style over Stojko's masculine, rock-star image, and that judges were turning a cold shoulder to the Canadian because his style was "controversial" or "ground-breaking." Not so on either account, according to international judges.

"If you were to look back at [Stojko's] last three world-championship performances, I think you would see a deterioration of style rather than a progression," said one world-level judge. "Choreography is part of the problem. Part of it is that, if you look at the Bruce Lee number [used to win his first world title in 1994], he started to show some line, some stretch, some class to the moves. This year, it wasn't there. . . . Many people have interpreted rough, tough, and nasty and have still showed some style."

Evgenia Shishkova and Vadim Naumov skate their exquisite short program to Bach's "Ave Maria." The couple won the short program at Skate Canada and earned a noisy, standing ovation from the Canadian audience. Shishkov was only sixty-two pounds (twenty-eight kilograms) and twelve years old when she was matched up with fifteen-year-old Naumov. On their first practice, they landed a triple throw. Both had previous pairs experience. "My old partner didn't jump very well," Naumov said. Shishkova and Naumov have been together for eleven years.

The 1984 Olympic champions Jayne Torvill and Christopher Dean worked as commentators for the Fox television network at the Champions Series final. Here, the couple, now professional ice dancers, do a routine to Art Garfunkel and Paul Simon's "Cecilia." Using this routine, Torvill and Dean (portraying a nerd in search of a date) won the world professional championship in Landover, Maryland, drawing four perfect marks of 10.

Sometimes, however, Stojko bends over at the waist while landing jumps such as the difficult triple Lutz. That's the kind of style shortcoming that judges use to place skaters, not the style of music used. "The European eye is much more in tune with [body style and line], because they see much more theater than a person does in North America," the judge explained. Interestingly enough, the judge who tied Urmanov and Stojko in the presentation marks was an American judge. "They don't have that same eye, which is why Americans don't do well in the dance competitions," the judge said.

Some judges and coaches also criticized the choreography of Stojko's short program, done to an auto-racing speedway theme. They looked askance at the simple forward stroking all the way down center ice during the opening seconds and at several moments where the skater moves his body while snapping his fingers – but all the while standing in one spot on the ice – and at spins placed inconspicuously at one end of the rink.

If the men's event offered much fodder for discussion or delight, the ice-dancing event in Paris was a bit of a yawn. In fact, ice dancing throughout the season failed to set dancing gurus afire. "I wouldn't say any of the free-dances were ones that would just make you die," said Ann Shaw, a Canadian who is a member of the International Skating Union's ice-dancing technical committee. "Grischuk and Platov won it, based on busy-ness of footwork rather than complexity of footwork, and the incredible speed with which they do things. I felt they were really good, but the vehicle could still be developed more. It's frantic and you can only take it so much. I'd say they were good and deserved to win, but I wouldn't say it was one of the more memorable free-dances."

Members of the ISU are hoping that dance goes in a different direction – back to skating and the use of edges. Many criticized Grischuk and Platov in 1995-96 for doing programs that so closely resembled some of their previous routines and were characterized by constant running steps.

"They seem to have gotten stuck in the fast and furious," says Joyce Hisey, an ISU council member. "They aren't really using edges, but the flat of the blade. They're looking like the successors to [1988 Olympic champions Natalia Bestemianova and Andrei Bukin], who were great entertainers and had lots of pizzazz, but if you look at their feet, they're not what you call overloaded with edges."

Hisey says that the improving Anjelika Krylova and Oleg Ovsiannikov may have more possibilities, but that Shae-Lynn Bourne and Victor Kraatz show a quality of edges that are "light years ahead of them."

"They have fantastic flow and glide, and their blade is just super on the ice. You're getting some skating when you look at Shae-Lynn and Victor. And I think [the Russians] should get into that kind of thing and they've sort of forgotten how."

Legendary British ice dancer and 1984 Olympic champion Christopher Dean, who watched the event from his perch at the Fox Network's commentators' booth in Paris, said he would like to see the top dancers offer more depth of expression. "I think there are extremely strong, physical skaters now, and, when you just see them warm up, they skate over the ice with tremendous speed," he said. "But I see a lot of exaggerated – almost too much, almost to the point of farcical – expression that is not believable. I'd like to see a little bit more depth and integrity come back. What they're doing is great, under the guidelines they've got, but I think they could all show more feeling.

"Grischuk and Platov are the leaders, and that's who everybody is following. I think they're very versatile skaters and, if they started to do other things, I think other people would follow." Just as many tried to follow Jayne Torvill and Christopher Dean after they skated in the glorious era of ice dancing. But two seasons before the 1998 Olympics, the current generation is still searching for a direction.

*T*he World Championship

*I*t is an event full of history – one hundred years of it. For amateur skaters, the world championship is the Stanley Cup, the Wimbledon crown, the NFL championship, all rolled into one. Although during the 1995-96 season the world championship offered prize money for the first time, it generally sets an amateur well on the way to top earning power in the professional world. Only Olympic gold is more highly prized and valued in the amateur skating world. The world championship took place in Edmonton, Alberta, from March 17 to 24.

Was the skate-off for medals at the world figure-skating championship in Edmonton so much different than that of the Champions Series final in Paris three weeks earlier? Yes. And no.

Exactly the same four ice-dancing and pairs teams competed. Yet the results differed, particularly in the pairs event, the most unpredictable of all disciplines. While Russians Marina Eltsova and Andrei Bushkov finished fourth and last after the short program in Paris, they astonishingly won the world title in a bizarre, error-marred contest.

Marina Anissina and Gwendal Peizerat stepped valiantly into the vacuum left by the injury of Sophie Moniotte, who, with Pascal Lavanchy, had been world silver medalists in 1994.

(Page 155) Oksana Grischuk and Evgeny Platov in their paso doble dance, considered the only male-centered dance in the discipline. Platov correctly shows the arrogant, intense attitude of the matador. Grischuk was a singles skater until she turned to dance at thirteen. "It was hard to change," she said. She became enthralled with dance when she saw the dramatic, expressive Soviet couple Irina Moiseeva and Andrei Minenkov, world champions in 1975 and 1977.

Takeshi Honda of Japan celebrated his fifteenth birthday while competing at the world championship in Edmonton. A student from Sendai City, Honda began skating only four years before becoming Japan's champion. Honda won one of the qualifying rounds in Edmonton, and finished thirteenth overall. The Japanese are touting him as a future world champion.

In Paris, the men's event lacked Rudy Galindo of the United States, who wasn't sent to any of the Champions Series qualifiers. He ended up winning the bronze medal in Edmonton. The women's event in Edmonton did not have Josée Chouinard of Canada, who won a bronze medal in Paris. And while the event in Paris was a pure, distilled version of the chase for gold in Edmonton, the world championship provided more drama down the line and a peek at future prowess: the delightful smile of Takeshi Honda of Japan, who turned fifteen the week of the world championship and landed two triple Axels in his long program to finish thirteenth; the awe-inspiring quadruple toe-loop–double toe-loop of sixteen-year-old Guo Zhengxin of China in his qualifying round (after a disastrous short program, Guo did not advance to the long program); the long-awaited return of Midori Ito of Japan, who faltered to finish seventh, obviously weakened by anemia in her rush back to the amateur wars; the return of a sleeker, rejuvenated Tanja Szewczenko of Germany, who finished sixth with six triples, a marvelous comeback after she was forced to withdraw the previous year with injuries; and little Tara Lipinski of the United States, astonishing in her virtuosity at age thirteen, landing a triple Salchow–triple loop jump, a combination

There are many who feel Midori Ito of Japan had no choice in reinstating as an amateur to compete at the 1998 Olympic Winter Games in her home country. Japanese officials in Edmonton said she missed competition and wanted to skate for Japan again. After she failed to win the 1992 Olympics, Ito apologized to the Japanese people. Some say Japanese journalists demanded the apology.

that wasn't seen even in the men's event and rarely seen at all. (The 1994 Olympic men's champion, Alexei Urmanov, stumbled out of his triple Salchow–double loop combination in the long program in Edmonton – and it was a rare combination.) Lipinski, adoring the spotlight, finished fifteenth over all, after a slow start in the short program.

What did it take to win a world title, the $50,000 (U.S.) first prize ($75,000 for pairs or dancers), and a prime spot on the long and lucrative Tom Collins Tour of World Champions that followed? The more triple jumps the better. A well-packaged program with expressive interpretation of music and choreography that included difficult steps between jumps ("The days of doing cross-cuts from end to end, and a long nothing before a jump are over," says ISU council member Joyce Hisey), and a minimum of mistakes. So competitive were the disciplines that mistakes became very costly.

Alexei Urmanov of Russia, Elvis Stojko of Canada, and Philippe Candeloro of France, the three men who stood on the podium at the 1994 Lillehammer Olympics, found out the hard way. They all made mistakes in Edmonton. They all missed the podium.

Stojko's error was the most shocking and unexpected; the crowd of seventeen thousand gasped in disbelief when the two-time world champion fell on a triple Axel that was supposed to be the first part of a triple toe-loop combination in the short program. The deductions were severe and, even though he skated one of the best long programs of his career, waving aside deep disappointment to land a quadruple-double combination and the triple-Axel combination that he had missed in the short program, he could pull up only to fourth place.

"Medals don't count," Stojko said bravely afterward. "You can't put a price on a performance. Men's skating is getting harder and harder. What took me out of the running was one jump.

"To bounce back from a [poor] performance teaches you so much. I learned a lifetime of things in the last two days."

Stojko said he actually was glad to be fourth, rather than third, because he will cherish his time atop podiums all the more – and want it back in the run-up to the Nagano Olympics.

Candeloro flopped dismally in the short program and dropped to sixteenth of twenty-nine men, but, after a strong skate in the long program, the French star managed to finish ninth overall.

Urmanov was in third place, within striking distance of gold after the short, but fell twice, staggered out of a combination during the long program, and dropped to fifth. He was disconsolate the following day. "Of course I'm sad," he said, the customary twinkle in his eye missing. "Next season will be even more difficult. Twice I have been fourth in the world, and now I am fifth. Elvis was fourth, but he was two-time world champion and he has to win again."

Fortunately, in spite of his fall from the medals, Urmanov got an invitation to travel on the Tom Collins tour throughout the United States. Otherwise, he would have had to go back to Russia homeless: his flat in St. Petersburg was being renovated for a month, perhaps two, and he had to move out.

Todd Eldredge had Rudy Galindo to thank – and he did, publicly – for losing the U.S. title he had already won three times and planting within him the gusto it took to come back and win the world title. Stojko applauded from the sidelines when he saw Eldredge landing everything in sight without a hitch, including the triple Axel–triple toe-loop combination he had missed at the Champions Series final. Eldredge got a standing ovation from the

Tanja Szewczenko,
back on track

*Philippe Candeloro
in his snake-man
costume, skating
to music from the
sci-fi movie* Dune.
*His fans did
not see his programs
until halfway through
the season as he
recovered from an
ankle injury suffered
during the Tom
Collins tour. "It was
not thought to be an
important injury, so
I kept training,"
Candeloro said.
"This was a mistake.
The doctor said I
would have to stop for
three weeks, but
when I came back
the injury was still
there. We had an
MRI done and it
showed some
ligament damage."
He had injections in
November. They
seemed to work, but
then Candeloro
began to have
problems with
his boots.*

spectators and first-place votes from five of the nine judges, just the majority he needed. Ilia Kulik of Russia won three, and Stojko was awarded the other from a Polish judge.

Ironically, Kulik had missed the draw for skating positions after winning the short program with his glorious speed and soft touch on the ice and the delicate landings of his picture-perfect triple jumps. Eldredge drew for him, and pulled out the last of twenty-four skating positions for the long. "I'll kill

Ilia Kulik in exhibition. Kulik was on pins and needles before the Russian federation finally decided to name him to the world-championship team. There were only two berths, but he finished third at the European championship (he had won it the previous year) and fourth of six at the Champions Series final. "I wasn't psychologically prepared," he said. However, showing brilliance, he won both the short and the long programs at the Centennial on Ice event in St. Petersburg, outfinishing Alexei Urmanov.

him," Kulik said jokingly at the time. "I don't like to skate last. It is half an hour after the warm-up. I have time to go to eat. It's awful."

Kulik, who admitted he was nervous before he skated the long, came very close to winning the event, only one season after he had won the world junior title; he is a major star in the making. The eighteen-year-old from Moscow missed the chance when he failed to land a second triple flip in combination. The flip survived, but, because Kulik had already done a triple flip earlier in the program, judges could give him no credit for it. (Rules dictate that a skater can repeat a triple jump only if it is part of a combination.) Kulik's miss gave Eldredge – and even Galindo – the edge on triples.

Michelle Kwan won the women's event in much the same way. Although defending champion Chen Lu of China showed a mature, beautiful sensitivity to every note and prompted a standing ovation from a crowd that chanted for perfect marks of 6.0, Kwan landed one more triple jump, with a grown-up will to win. When Kwan failed to do an ambitious triple toe-loop–triple toe-loop combination in the long program (she did a triple-double), she threw in an extra triple toe-loop at the end of her program. Chen was forced to settle for the silver medal, in spite of a superb performance.

Michelle Kwan in victory – as usual

Chen Lu's downfall also perhaps occurred because of the quality of her spins: she barely did two rotations on a camel spin, only about one and a half rotations for each position in her combination spin, and displayed no real sit spin at all. Judges who were watching this were probably very mindful of a proposed amendment to skating rules that would stipulate a minimum of four rotations in long-program spins. This amendment would have been fresh in judges' minds when they watched Chen; they would have received notice of proposed changes only a week or two before the Edmonton event. These technical items sealed Kwan's win with six of the nine judges; the other three thought Chen's exquisite performance was still better, regardless. When Kwan won, it was the sixth time in eight years that a skater of Asian heritage had won the women's event.

Irina Slutskaia of Russia also outpointed her compatriot Maria Butyrskaia and won the bronze medal with an arsenal of triples, landing six of them (some in difficult combinations) to Butyrskaia's five. The women's event was one of the most competitive and cleanly skated in memory.

"I could see fire in [Kwan's] face," said 1976 Olympic bronze medalist Toller Cranston, who watched the event. "In spite of the hair and the fancy clothes, she's a tough, little, feisty competitor. She's got spirit. I think Frank

Carroll plays a major role in her making. She is totally devoted to him. If he were to ask her to jump off the CN Tower, she would. That kind of loyalty brings success."

Clearly, the Russians and the Americans were best at keeping up to the increasing demand for difficulty, while France and Canada faltered. The Russians and Americans fielded the largest teams of sixteen athletes, but, in the medal count, the Russians fared slightly better, with two gold, two silver, and one bronze. The Americans picked up two gold and two bronzes; but it was an amazing turnaround from the world championship of 1993, when no Americans made it to the podium.

"In 1993, everybody was predicting the end of the American team," said David Dore, director-general of the Canadian Figure Skating Association. "Look where they are today. You can be here today and gone tomorrow. It's that quick. The Russians still have a strong base. Obviously, when they have had coaches that have left for other countries, they've had equally qualified coaches to replace them.

"And the Americans have had such success in singles because their culture is a little more aggressive than ours. Perhaps our skaters are holding back a bit."

In Edmonton, the United States had three men finish in the top ten (Daniel Hollander, the U.S. bronze medalist, ill with the flu in the days leading up to the world championship, still finished tenth), and two women in the top ten – all in all with two gold medalists in the singles events. Russians won gold in the other two disciplines.

Still, the United States had its pairs team of Jenni Meno and Todd Sand win the bronze medal, even without doing a triple jump, while the vastly improved Elizabeth Punsalan and Jerod Swallow finished seventh in ice dancing, their best result in that discipline in many years. Punsalan and Swallow had not even made it to the world championship the previous year.

France, which has been a figure-skating power since the 1992 Albertville Olympics, earning one silver and two bronzes in 1995, was completely and soundly shut out of podium positions in Edmonton. It didn't help that its ice-dancing medalists from the previous two years, Sophie Moniotte and Pascal Lavanchy, missed the entire season after Moniotte broke her ankle.

France's poor finish had team director Didier Gailhaguet strongly suggesting that Suzanne Bonaly hang up her coaching hat and allow someone else to train her daughter, Surya, who finished only fifth, missing the podium

Maria Butryskaia
lets her hair down
in exhibitions.

for the first time in four years. After Bonaly met with disaster in the short program and slipped to seventh, her mother steered her away from any probing reporters, including those from the French network TF1, which had paid $200,000 (U.S.) a year for priority interviewing rights. The French media threw up their hands in frustration in Edmonton.

"It's all happened since the Albertville Games," said Paul Peret, a French reporter with the European Broadcasting Union. "Her mother doesn't want her to give interviews. The mother is responsible for that, not Surya. I think it is a nightmare."

Peret said a colleague in France, who was attempting to interview Surya, faced such roadblocks that he was forced to send his questions via fax to the

Some of the French media have been waiting for four years to get an interview with Surya Bonaly of France. French broadcast reporter Paul Peret blames Bonaly's adoptive mother, Suzanne. "What doesn't her mother control?" he said. "I think it's a nightmare for the girl. Suzanne says every day that Surya's the best skater in the world. It's never her fault when she doesn't win. It's usually because there's something wrong with her boots."

family compound. Bonaly replied by fax, but, Peret said, "You know who wrote the answers."

Mother Bonaly, who is a physical-education teacher, is well known for her program of tough practice drills: Surya often skates full out during entire practices, and rarely does two competitions in a season when five will do. During the 1995-96 season, Bonaly appeared burned out, with few strong performances. French pairs skater Stéphane Bernadis found out how intensely Coach Bonaly drives practices when he skated pairs with Surya one summer, before he was matched up with his current partner, Sarah Abitbol.

"It was hard," he said. "[Surya] skated many hours a day, and I had to do the same, because of her mother. It was not the same as human."

Even Chinese coach Li Mingzhu watched the Bonalys in wonder. "Her mother pushes her too much," she said. "She needs a rest."

With both Canada and France fighting for a medal – any kind of medal – the battle came down to the ice-dancing event, traditionally Canada's weakest discipline, but a strong event for France ever since Isabelle and Paul Duchesnay won the 1991 world championship. (Ironically, the Duchesnays were Canadians who ended up skating for France.) In Edmonton, France and Canada ended up scrambling for the same face-saving medal, but the home team won out, as Canadian champions Shae-Lynn Bourne and Victor Kraatz overturned fast-rising French skaters Marina Anissina and Gwendal Peizerat to win the bronze medal.

The French and the Canadians had been trading victories all year. They met at Skate Canada, while Bourne was limping and skating stiffly with seventeen stitches in her knee from an injury that occurred the Friday before the event, when Kraatz accidently brought a foot down during a helicopter move and slashed his partner's leg. The Canadians narrowly won the original dance, the *paso doble*, over the French, but a French fall during the free-dance assured victory for the ailing Canadians.

However, Anissina and Peizerat had moved ahead of the Canadians during the original dance at the NHK Trophy and eventually won gold, upsetting the Canadians, who had been ranked two spots ahead of them at the 1995 world championship. Anissina and Peizerat had also defeated them at the Champions Series final, leaving Bourne and Kraatz's stylist, Uschi Keszler, near tears. She claimed that judges were trying to mold her skaters into their image and thereby infringing on the skaters' human rights. "I've been asking for an explanation, but all they tell us is that we don't interpret the rules the way they want us to," Keszler said.

Canadian officials thought otherwise. "They didn't have enough difficulty [in both the original dance and free-skate]," said ISU council member and ice-dancing aficionado Joyce Hisey. "They had the wrong concept for the *paso doble*. They felt that everybody else was doing the rather dramatic, dynamic interpretation, and they were going to do something different. But their something different didn't have the characteristics of a true *paso doble*, which is dramatic and quick and sharp and precise. The character wasn't appropriate to the rhythm chosen."

Kurt Browning was left to perform with singing star Michael Burgess after the ISU forbade him – as a pro skater – to perform in the opening ceremonies.

Olympic ice-dancing champion Christopher Dean was impressed with what he saw while watching Canadians Shae-Lynn Bourne and Victor Kraatz at the Champions Series final. "Bourne and Kraatz have a very organic way of skating," he said. "They use the ice and the edges. They have deep, strong edges, whereas Grischuk and Platov tend to skate over the ice, turning and twisting. Bourne and Kraatz skate into the ice."

It was clear that drastic action was needed. Within ten days before the world championship, Russian coach Natalia Dubova, who had been working with the Canadians on technique, overhauled their programs, according to officials. The former coach of 1992 Olympic ice-dancing champions Marina Klimova and Sergei Ponomarenko – who coached Bourne and Kraatz in 1994-95 – took a new piece of music for the *paso doble* and recreated the attitude of their dance. Lawrence Demmy, the first vice-president of the ISU and a four-time world ice-dancing champion for Britain, said he was amazed at the changes wrought in so short a time.

Dubova also added a tremendous amount of footwork and different dance-hold positions to the free-dance. "We were all aware that they had the ability to do it," Hisey said. "They just had the incorrect vehicle."

Bourne and Kraatz worked diligently for their bronze, the first world ice-dancing medal Canada has earned since Tracy Wilson and the late Robert McCall won bronze in 1988. "They worked like dogs," Hisey said. "They spent hours in Lake Placid, until one and two in the morning. I commend them. They deserved that medal."

About two weeks after the world championship, Bourne and Kraatz left Keszler, saying that they wanted to concentrate their training in one spot – Lake Placid, New York – rather than shifting between that town and Philadelphia, where Keszler is based. Dubova will remain as their technical coach.

If the ice-dancing event was predictable at the very top – Grischuk and Platov won their third consecutive world title, while promising training mates Anjelika Krylova and Oleg Ovsiannikov won silver, exactly their placing at the Champions Series final – the pairs event was not. In fact, it was a disappointment, with much flawed skating. And the skaters drew a most intriguing set of ordinals or placements that produced rather unexpected world champions in Marina Eltsova and Andrei Bushkov of Russia.

Evgenia Shishkova and Vadim Naumov of Russia, who were favored to win after taking the Champions Series final and everything else they contested this year, finished fourth, even though they had four first-place votes from nine judges in the long, just short of winning the majority of judges' hearts. Eltsova and Bushkov also drew four first-place marks after skating the most error-free and difficult program, but they did not have a majority either, because the other first-place mark went to German skaters Mandy Woetzel and Ingo Steuer. (That mark came, not surprisingly, from a German judge.)

ISU president Ottavio Cinquanta finally was cheered when he allowed Kurt Browning to skate in the closing ceremonies.

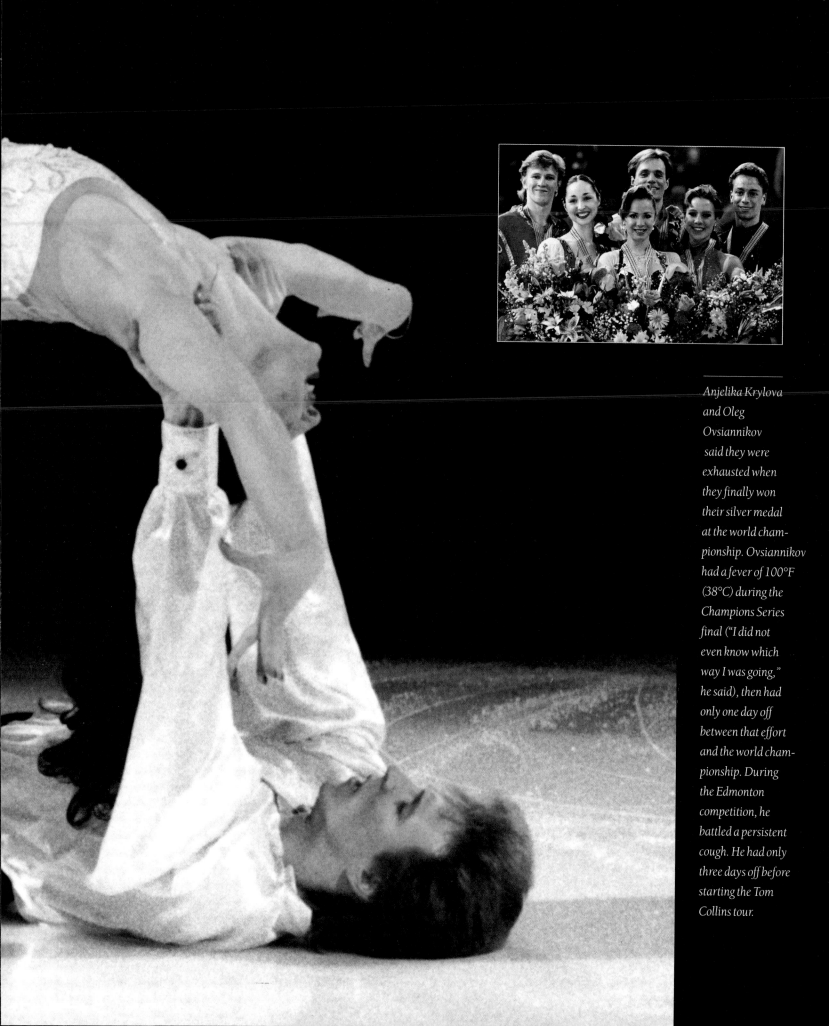

Anjelika Krylova
and Oleg
Ovsiannikov
said they were
exhausted when
they finally won
their silver medal
at the world cham-
pionship. Ovsiannikov
had a fever of 100°F
(38°C) during the
Champions Series
final ("I did not
even know which
way I was going,"
he said), then had
only one day off
between that effort
and the world cham-
pionship. During
the Edmonton
competition, he
battled a persistent
cough. He had only
three days off before
starting the Tom
Collins tour.

Marina Eltsova and Andrei Bushkov of Russia won a gold world medal after they left famous Russian coach Igor Moskvin. Moskvin never considered himself to be wrong, Bushkov once told a reporter. In 1992, Moskvin changed Bushkov's boot and blade only two days before a Skate Canada competition. When Bushkov fell many times at Skate Canada, Moskvin told him he didn't know how to skate. After the 1995 world championship, in which they finished fourth, Moskvin's wife, Tamara, advised them to become pros. The pair felt unwanted, but responded by changing coaches and winning gold.

Officials had to look to second-place ordinals to find a winner. Because Shishkova and Naumov had a sprinkling of fourths and a third, Eltsova and Bushkov took the win with two second-place ordinals. Woetzel and Steuer won the silver, and Jenni Meno and Todd Sand, who took the bronze for the United States, had no first-place ordinals at all, but still finished ahead of Shishkova and Naumov, the 1994 world champions, because the Americans had more second- and third-place votes.

The race for pairs medals in Edmonton was supposed to be a contest of triple jumps, the most recent trend in the risky discipline since the International Skating Union allowed them in the short program two years before. In

Edmonton, sixteen of twenty-three pairs tried a triple jump in the short program. Only seven succeeded.

Among the misses were all of the Russians: Shishkova and Eltsova both needed to put their second foot down on the landing of triple toe-loops to avoid falling, while Oksana Kazakova, teamed for the first time with the wildly artistic and arresting Artur Dmitriev, fell on her attempt and ended up fifth overall. Canadian silver medalists Kristy Sargeant and Kris Wirtz were one of the seven pairs to succeed with the jump in the short program; they finished seventh overall.

But in short, the pairs event was disappointing: too many mistakes and not enough of that extra performance level that Olympic champions Ekaterina Gordeeva and the late Sergei Grinkov had in abundance. "They were almost untouchable," said Barbara Underhill, a former world pairs champion for Canada with Paul Martini. "They had an ethereal quality about them. That's what missing with other teams, that magic. All of the teams at the top have one thing that is lacking.

Eltsova and Bushkov,
bucking the odds

"But in pairs skating, so much is required now that it's tough to have absolutely everything. It's very obvious now that pairs skaters have to be jumpers, too. It puts so much pressure on them that wasn't there before. And very few of them can land them yet. We're seeing a lot more mistakes in the programs."

Kazakova and Dmitriev have the magic and intensity, Underhill said, but they have been together too short a time to gel as a unit and to iron out all of the tough competitive kinks. Shishkova and Naumov are "wonderful to watch and technically very strong, but not exciting," she said. "They don't set me on the edge of my seat."

Eltsova and Bushkov made a valiant attempt to find the magic by dropping their famous coach, Igor Moskvin, coach of the legendary Olympic champions Ludmila and Oleg Protopopov, and executing softer, more-lyrical programs that show increased communication between the two to add to their strong technical abilities.

Woetzel and Steuer, always mechanical and cool in a contemporary way in the past, took a major step forward this year by getting world silver medalist ice dancers Susanna Rahkamo and Petri Kokko of Finland to choreograph their programs. "They have the short program of the year," Underhill said. "But sometimes they seem to get so stiff, and [Mandy] doesn't look comfortable sometimes."

Mandy Woetze
and Ingo Steue
were rather cre
fallen about the
efforts in finish
second at the w
championship.
They had overc
much: injuries
throughout the
season and cold
during the wee
the world event
And they drew
dreaded numbe
one starting pos
for the short pro
at Edmonton. I
spite of it all, th
won the short
program. They
made a flurry
of mistakes in t
long program,
then so did man
others. On a m
prone night, We
and Steuer wer
second-best.

Of the group, Meno and Sand were flawless in Edmonton, leaving coach John Nicks puzzled about their placement, but the American couple did not attempt triple jumps in either the short or the long program. "Their program gives you goose bumps, but technically they are not strong," Underhill said, referring to their simple jumps and their triple twist, in which Sand often fails to catch his partner before she lands back on the ice.

The trend in pairs skating is so clear that Canadian coach Paul Wirtz said he has already begun to push his team, Sargeant and Wirtz (his younger brother), into practicing some of the most difficult triples, flips, and Lutzes. "You might realistically need a triple flip by 1998," he said. Currently, pairs skaters are doing the two easiest triples, the toe loop and Salchow, although third-ranked U.S. team Shelby Lyons and Brian Wells attempted difficult triple loops in competitions in 1995-96. (Lyons landed hers in the long program in Edmonton, but Wells put a hand to the ice to regain his balance.)

In Edmonton, it was clear that the technical stakes will be high in the future, but even that is not enough. Canadian pairs champions Michelle Menzies and Jean-Michel Bombardier are already incorporating dance steps into their programs, choreographed by Marina Zoueva, the stylist for Gordeeva and Grinkov. In a way, all skaters are on a quest to recreate and celebrate the perfection of the esteemed Russian pair.

After All

Quietly, but emphatically, International Skating Union judges left a lasting, important message during the 1995-96 season. And it was there for all to see – in their presentation marks.

For the first time, the judges made obvious deductions from presentation marks (or, in long programs, gave significant credit for artistry well performed). Although the ISU had been urging such deductions or credits for the past few years, it began to stress them more pointedly during this season after a series of judges' committee meetings. In the past, the presentation marks appeared to be tied closely to the technical ones; there was often little difference between them.

The presentation mark has become important in ice dancing, because, in recent years, there has been more of an emphasis on free-skating rather than on the technical compulsory dances. Over the past several years, ice dancers have been required to do only two, instead of three, compulsories in competitions, and for certain events this season (Skate America, the Champions Series final), only one. Also, starting with the 1994-95 season, judges have awarded two sets of marks for technical merit and presentation for compulsory dances – rather than only a single mark that incorporated both. Along with that change, skating in time to the music became a vital part of the presentation mark. "You want to give skaters credit if they have very

Steven Cousins's popular exhibition routine used his outgoing, playful personality to advantage. The skater from Britain attained his greatest achievement — and yet one of his most frustrating — by finishing fourth at the European championship in Sofia, Bulgaria. A seven-time British champion who trains alongside Elvis Stojko in Canada, Cousins said he felt "gutted, absolutely gutted" by his failure to win a medal. No British man had won any color of medal since Robin Cousins (no relation) won the event in 1980. Steven Cousins had been in third place after the short program, but fell on a triple Axel in the long. "But I'm definitely going to be taken seriously now," he said.

(Page 177 and facing page) Ilia Kulik

Surya Bonaly came to life during her exhibition routine at the world championship. Winning standing ovations, Bonaly chucked her glitter-laden costumes for simple and powerful leopard skin. Here, she is midway through one of her famous one-footed back flips. During the summer of 1996, Bonaly damaged an Achilles tendon, a serious injury that is expected to put her out of action for four months.

simplistic footwork, but fabulous artistry," said one international official. "But you want it to work in the reverse as well for programs that are complex, but 'boring as hell.'"

This season, the move affected singles skaters, too: Surya Bonaly of France; to a minor extent Irina Slutskaia of Russia; Viacheslav Zagorodniuk of Ukraine; Philippe Candeloro of France; and Guo Zhengxin of China. It affected Elvis Stojko of Canada markedly. All but one of his presentation marks for the long program at the world championship in Edmonton were lower than his technical marks. It cost him the Champions Series final, too, in a similar scenario in Paris. What might the judges have been seeing?

Presentation (formerly called artistic impression) involves eight major areas of a program: harmonious composition (the skater has to conform to what the music is asking); speed and variation of speed; use of the ice surface (the skater has to have a well-balanced program, with jumps and other elements well laid out over the ice, changes of direction, use of curves and choreography that does not allow the skater to spend too much time, for example, dancing in one spot); easy movement and sureness in time to the music (basic, good-quality skating that flows freely through direction changes and footwork); carriage and style (the skater's freeleg should show good extension, toes should be pointed, and, overall, a skater should show beautiful body movements that include the head and the arms – a judge does not want to see a skater forgetting fineness of carriage while preparing for a jump); originality (the choice of music doesn't matter, but the choreography and the musical response to it does); expression of the character of the music; and, when two people are skating together on the ice, stroking technique, body lean, and body line must be in unison.

There are other considerations, too, for skaters at the very top: in the judges eyes, they have to demonstrate a range of artistic ability. "You get the same bunch of judges, year after year, particularly in Europe, where a country might have only one or two world judges," said one world-level judge. "So they become very familiar with people's work. . . . The mark of a true athlete is the ability to take your skating and change the style to do something with it. Kurt Browning was probably the best we've ever seen, if you think of the huge range of different things he's done. That ability to take his skating and completely modify it to the needs of the particular performance is the mark of a real top skater. None of the men we had in worlds this year matched that kind of ability."

All skaters are, to a certain extent, limited. Few excel at all of the presentation areas laid out by the ISU. Alexei Urmanov, praised for his line and style, works with a somewhat limited repertoire of classical music, which nevertheless has great potential to evoke all kinds of feelings and emotions. The 1992 Olympic champion Victor Petrenko of Ukraine was even more restricted in his program choices. He used a narrow range of classical music, allowing Browning to defeat him time and again. With all of these thoughts in mind, many judges at the top are concerned that Stojko is unable to break out of his masculine, techno mold.

"They're starting to say, 'What else have you got?'" the judge said. "His moves are generic. They're taking music that fits his style, rather than pushing him to grow. There is a feeling in the skating world that, if you're not growing, you're stagnating."

If one male skater showed enormous potential in the area of presentation, it was Ilia Kulik of Russia, a skater who mixed music from the popular world – *The Addams Family* and *Aladdin* soundtracks – with mesmerizing arm movements, body line, and ballet-dance style. And there is a glimmer of sharp-witted humor about him that shows up in his exhibitions. It is this kind of style and flexibility that wins world and Olympic gold – especially in the brave new world of figure skating, where audience appeal helps, but artistry wins the day. It is the real world.

A C K N O W L E D G E M E N T S

Authors never work in complete isolation, and that is why I can never possibly thank all of the people who have contributed in so many ways to this volume. But special thanks to the following:

Marina Zoueva, who opened up her heart;

Dwayne, Hu, and all the rest at the muscle shop. Without their help, I would not have been able to write this book;

Alex Graf, a television producer from Beijing, who went out of his way to help break down barriers;

Yossi Goldberg, who first opened the door to Israel for me;

Donald Jackson, who jumped in to help at a moment's notice;

Sharon Lariviere, who greatly went out of her way to pick up a weary author at a hotel, take her home, and show her home movies of China, all in cheery fashion;

Don Laws, for his generous, kind help and his postal epistles;

Li Mingzhu, who made time for a long, interesting, candid chat;

Eli Rubenstein, for his generous help in all things Israel;

Edith Smith, who always had her finger on the VCR buttons;

Fred Lum, for his unwavering moral support;

Bruce Westwood, for smoothing the way;

Pat Kennedy, Kong, Heather Sangster, and all the rest at my publishing family, McClelland & Stewart.

PHOTO CREDITS

INDEX